404359

BOUND & DETERMINED

A VISUAL HISTORY OF
CORSETS
1850–1960

KRISTINA SELESHANKO

D1612523

DOVER PUBLICATIONS, INC.
MINEOLA, NEW YORK

university for the **creative arts**

Rochester
Ford Pitt
Rochester
Kent
ME1 1DZ

Tel: 01634 888734
e-mail: libraryroch@ucreative.ac.uk

Bibliographical Note

Bound & Determined: A Visual History of Corsets, 1850–1960 is a new work,
first published by Dover Publications, Inc., in 2012.

International Standard Book Number
ISBN-13: 978-0-486-47892-0
ISBN-10: 0-486-47892-0

Manufactured in the United States by Courier Corporation
47892001
www.doverpublications.com

Introduction

It is the lesser blot, modesty finds,
Women to change their shapes, than men their minds.
—William Shakespeare, *Two Gentlemen of Verona*

"One of the highest entertainments in Turkey is having you go to their baths," aristocrat Lady Mary Wortley Montagu wrote in an 1850s edition of *Godey's Lady's Book*. "When I was first introduced to one, the lady of the house came to undress me—another high compliment they pay to strangers. After she slipped off my gown and my stays, she was very much struck by the sight of them and cried out to the ladies in the bath, 'Come hither, and see how cruelly the poor English ladies are used by their husbands. You need not boast, indeed, of the superior liberties allowed to you when they lock you up in a box.'"

The "box," which every American woman from colonial days through the 1950s came gift wrapped in, was the corset. To modern women, the idea of keeping house, shopping, rearing children, dancing, and even swimming and playing sports— all while barely able to bend over in a corset— seems impossible and even ridiculous. Why did women do that to themselves? we wonder.

The answer heard most often is vanity. Then, as now, few women were satisfied with their natural figure. Corsets were the only means of obtaining the currently-popular shape, whether it was the rigidly flat torso and raised bosom of the seventeenth century, the flat-stomached, high-busted, shoulders-back look of the eighteenth century, or the hourglass figure of the nineteenth century. In the early- and mid-twentieth century, corsets worked something like a rigid diet and hours in the gym do today, flattening the stomach and hips, and often trimming the waistline, too.

While many women did wear corsets for vanity, there were other reasons for putting on a corset. Bras didn't become popular until the 1930s, so corsets acted as a bosom support. Also, during many eras, women's clothes were skin tight; without a corset, bodices would have constantly wrinkled and ridden up.

Corsets also affected a woman's demeanor. As one Victorian mother wrote to a fashion magazine, at first her daughter rejected "the discipline of the corset" but now "her only objection is that the corsets are uncomfortable and prevent her from romping about..." Which was exactly the point. Corsets altered more than the figure; they also affected the behavior and, it was believed, the character of the women who wore them.

Dress reformer Helen Gilbert Ecob, in her 1892 book *The Well Dressed Woman*, mentions this argument. She wrote: "Those who uphold the corset argue its morality because 'the only period in which its general use appears to have been discontinued are the few years which immediately followed the French Revolution, when the general licentiousness of manners and morals was accompanied by a corresponding indecency in dress.'"

And to a great many women, not wearing a corset did seem indecent. Corsets in one form or another had been around since biblical times, and were adopted by nearly all women by the sixteenth century. Ecob claimed that by 1892 American women bought 60,000,000 corsets each year. After generations of dedicated corset wearing, many women were uncomfortable going without—as if they were walking around naked.

Corsets always had their detractors. In the early days of corset wearing, many people condemned them as the artifice they were. Pastors and priests considered them a rejection of the naturally beautiful figure God gave woman, in addition to a device meant to snare men by calling attention to female sexuality.

Havelock Ellis, an early sexologist (who was himself sexually dysfunctional), wrote in 1923 that one of the main attractions of the corset was that it caused women to breathe in a shallow manner. This, in turn drew greater attention to the breasts, because they moved up and down in a more conspicuous manner. He also claimed he knew women who said they were in a constant state of arousal when they were tight laced.

Letters to the editor from the 1800s also show that some people found corsets sexual. One Victorian man wrote to a fashion magazine: "There is something to me extraordinarily fascinating in the thought that a young girl has for many years been subjected to the strictest discipline of the corset. If she has suffered, as I have no doubt she has...it must be quite made up to her by the admiration her figure excited."

During the nineteenth century, doctors and laymen began suspecting a connection between women's notoriously delicate health and corset wearing. "What a host of evils follows in the steps of tight-lacing," Victorian author Mary P. Merrifield wrote, "indigestion, hysteria, spinal curvature, liver complaints, disease of the heart, cancer, early death!" The further the century progressed, the more the evils of the corset were accepted as fact. Yet women continued corseting!

Some persistence in wearing corsets was due to ignorance. "We have just received a letter," wrote the editor of *Dress* in 1888, "in which the writer declares that a woman's waist, left to itself, will grow larger and larger every year, until it measures nearly or quite as much as the bust!"

But there's little doubt corset wearing also continued due to a desire for a new style under-garment that could both support the figure *and* make women feel less naked than they would sans corset. Corsets were so firmly entrenched in feminine life, it seemed impossible to live without them.

Babies and young children wore felt "bands" or "waists" to keep their chests warm. Girls as young as four wore training corsets, usually stiffened with cording. By the time a girl was twelve to fourteen, she could expect to graduate to a full-fledged corset. There were rust-proof corsets for swimming, short corsets for horseback riding, corsets with elastic inserts to make housekeeping chores easier, "electric" corsets that replaced whalebone with magnetic strips and claimed to "ward off and cure diseases," nursing corsets, maternity corsets—a corset for every occasion. No wonder it seemed impossible to live without them!

"What is most singular is that women are aware of the injuriousness of the corset—they instinctively feel that its action is an unnatural and eminently hurtful one," a medical doctor wrote to *Godey's Lady's Book* in the 1860s. "Here is the proof. If...a lady falls ill in a crowded assembly of any kind, a general cry is raised by the others, 'Cut her lace!' This is done instantly—the compressing machine is opened, air rushes into the lungs, the victim breathes and recovers."

Yet the discomfort of the corset wasn't just due to restrictiveness. According to author Helen Gilbert Ecob, Dr. Robert L. Dickinson of Brooklyn conducted scientific studies showing just how much pressure corsets put on women's bodies, publishing his findings in an 1887 issue of the *New York Medical Journal*. The most physical pressure the doctor measured from a corset was eighty-eight pounds. "The pressure of a loose corset," Ecob reported, "is about thirty-five pounds." As she then points out, few women could lift a common sack of flour, yet "a sack of flour weighs twenty-five pounds—ten pounds less than the pressure of the loosest corset."

Ecob also reported that corsets caused the floating ribs to squeeze inward "until they nearly meet in the centre." In corset wearers, Ecob wrote, the upper ribs were raised and expanded wider than in a person who didn't wear corsets.

Because of pressure on the diaphragm and changes to the rib cage, Dr. Dickinson estimated a corseted woman's lung power was reduced by one fifth. He was forward-thinking, because it wasn't until the turn of the century that doctors agreed that women and men actually breathed in the same fashion. Before this time, many physicians believed female breathing changed naturally at puberty—apparently not realizing the onset of puberty also brought about snug corsets for girls.

Dr. J. H. Kellogg, best known for creating Corn Flakes cereal but also an influential doctor at the turn of the century, was famous for condemning the corset. In his 1895 book *Ladies' Guide*, he retells several extreme stories about tight lacing. For example, he mentions reading in a newspaper "of a young woman who actually broke a rib in the attempt to gain another half-inch on her corset string," and says that "more than one case is on record of young ladies who have applied the belt or corset so tightly that a blood-vessel has been ruptured and almost instant death has occurred."

Despite these famous and dire stories, Victorian fashion magazines are full of letters written by women bragging about their tightly corseted waistlines. Some women claimed waists as small as 13 inches, yet Doris Langely Moore, costume expert and founder of Bath's Museum of Costume, proclaimed it rare to find 19th-century women's dresses with waistlines less than 20 inches. Most likely, she said, Victorian women were referring to their corset size, not their actual waist measurement. When properly worn, the back edges of a corset did not meet, leaving a gap of at least two—and sometimes as much as 5 or 6—inches. Therefore, a woman bragging of her 17 inch corset would have had a corseted waist measuring anywhere from 19 to 22 inches. Even so, some period photographs reveal extreme cases where women's waists are clearly much smaller than this.

Nonetheless, by the early 1900s, women were concerned enough about corsets to adopt the "health corset." Originally designed by a corsetiere with a degree in medicine, this new-style corset was designed to put less pressure on vital organs. When snugly laced, however, the corset threw the hips back and the bust forward, creating the odd but fashionable S-shape figure of the era.

When clothes began growing snug in the 1910s, the corset grew longer and more ungainly, making movement more difficult than ever, until corsets were abandoned altogether in the 1920s. Or so fashion designers led women to believe. The introduction of elastic in 1911 and the shortage of both whalebone and metal at this time didn't, in fact, banish the corset—but both instances did allow designers to give the corset a much overdue remake.

The new corsets were not made of unbending whalebone, steel, and stiff cloth; they were more flexible and made with plenty of elastic and feather boning. They were also given a new name: Girdles.

No longer was fashion's emphasis on curving figures. Now a leaner look was desirable. "You can't have any bulges in your figure," the editors of a 1933 issue of *Vogue* warned. This was a look corsets couldn't create, but which girdles were ideal for.

Some wonder why women of the 1920s through 1960s didn't just eat better and exercise more, thereby avoiding the discomfort and complexity of the girdle. A 1932 issue of *Vogue* gives the answer: "A women's abdominal muscles are notoriously weak, and even hard exercise doesn't keep your figure from spreading if you don't give it some support." In other words, even diet and exercise couldn't give most women the smooth, lean look demanded by fashion during this period.

Now and then, true corsets reappeared. The 1940s saw fashions inspired by the late Victorians, and with them some "waist-whittlers" were sold. After WWII, English designer Christian Dior famously introduced his "New Look," and with it came the "waspie." A short corset about 5 or 6 inches long, made of stiff fabric with elastic inserts, boning, and back laces, the waspie was truly a mini version of a Victorian corset.

During the 1950s, when designers reintroduced feminine curves and girdles, corsets and long line bras worked to whittle the waist and make the bust and hips look more rounded. Girdle makers also created designs just for mature or stout women;

these looked more like traditional corsets but were given more innocuous names, like "corslets."

And while the hourglass figure hasn't been in fashion since that time, corsets still appear in fashion now and then—usually as outwear for evening and bridal gowns, but also as sexy underwear. In fact, what was once an underground movement of closet tight-lacers has grown into a trend that's made corset-making a profitable business again. Thousands of catalogs feature modern corsets of nearly any description.

As for girdles—they never really went out of style. Support top pantyhose were the girdles of choice in the 1970s, but from the 1980s forward, girdles in the form of "support wear" became fashionable. True, few modern women wear girdles every day, but department stores still carry racks of them for special occasions. Although women have "come a long way, baby," it seems our figures still disappoint us.

Making Corsets

Rigid boning, complicated seams, all those eyelets… many people find corset-making intimidating. But the truth is, most corsets aren't all that difficult to sew. For a first attempt, it's a good idea to stick with a fairly simple pattern, like a short Victorian corset in a size that's about 3 inches smaller than the wearer's actual bust, waist, and hip measurements.

Although the exterior of the corset can be any type of fabric, the layer of fabric closest to the skin should be quite strong. Coutil is generally the fabric of choice; it's readily available online from costume and corset-making websites.

The type of ultra-flexible, light plastic boning sold in the average fabric store chain won't work well for corseting. An online costume supply store selling corset making supplies is a better source. Flat steel boning is the most rigid type, but it's still flexible enough for comfort. It comes in a wide variety of lengths—and usually several lengths are required for making a single corset. Spiral steel boning is another good choice; it's more flexible still, but can still shape the body. It's also possible to cut spiral bones with wire cutters, making them exactly the length required. Special caps are then placed over the cut edges.

Most corsets close in front with a stomach-flattening steel busk. These feature special hook closures that make getting in and out of the corset easier. Costuming stores carry many styles of busks, in addition to metal eyelets (grommets) and tools for attaching them to fabric. (Eyelets can also be sewn by hand, and many sewing machines feature a special setting for sewing eyelets.)

Here's how the average corset is created: Each side of the corset is constructed by taking two layers of fabric (for example, strong coutil and decorative brocade) and sewing them together, wrong sides together, along the front opening. One half of the busk is slipped into place along each side of this front opening, with holes cut out so the special busk clasps can protrude from the fabric.

Channels for inserting the bones are sewn next, often by stitching lines down the length of the corset, through both layers of fabric. (Alternatively, binding is sewn to the lining fabric.) Eyelets or grommets are added to the back edges of the corset. The bottom and top edges of the corset are finished with binding. Finally, a single, long piece of cording is used to lace up the corset in the back. Two large loops of cording are left at the waist, to make waist nipping easy.

—*Kristina Seleshanko*

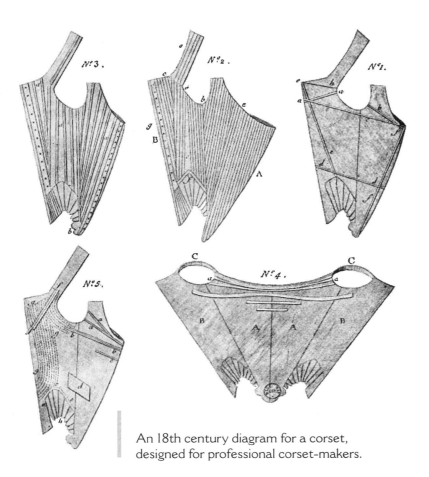

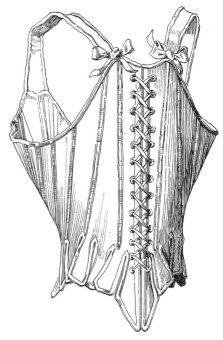

Corsets of the 18th century took time to get into. The shoulder straps always tied in place—often in the back—and the laces (often in the back or on each side) required assistance to lace.

An 18th century diagram for a corset, designed for professional corset-makers.

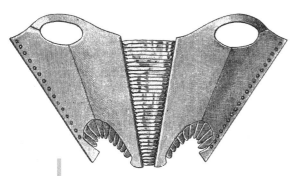

An illustration of a corset from the *Encyclopédie de Diderot*, published between 1751 and 1772.

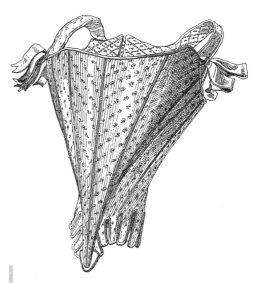

The flaps on the bottom of these 18th century stays added a small amount of roundness to the hips and allowed for the use of panniers or hoops.

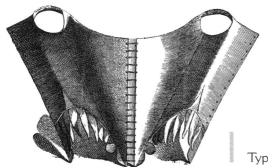

Typical 18th century stays.

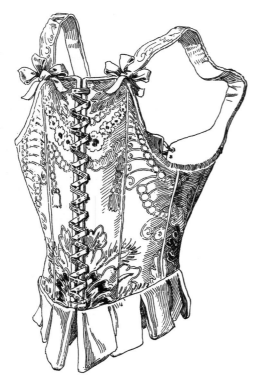

Corsets for the wealthy were often quite beautiful. This 18th century corset appears to be made from brocade.

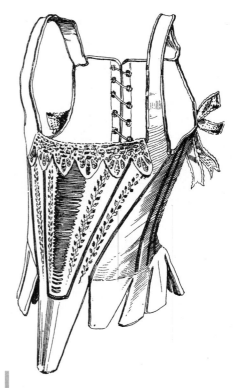

An early 18th century pair of stays.

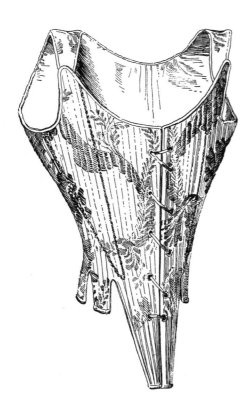

Stays from the 18th century were less about cinching in the waist and more about flattening the stomach and pushing up the bust.

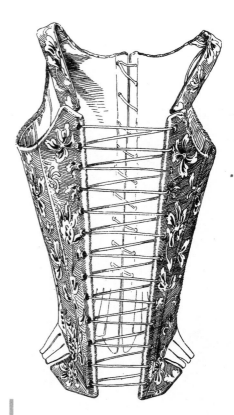

Stays with front and back lacing.

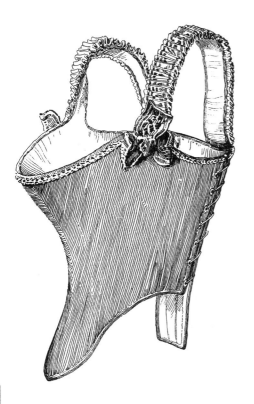

Stays with ruched ribbon shoulder straps.

These stays were for a nursing mother.

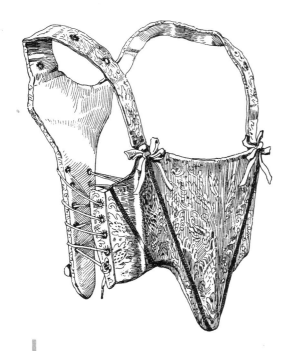

These short stays had eyelets that allow the bodice to attach to the corset's shoulder straps.

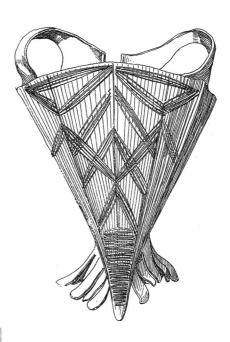

A great deal of time and money was sometimes spent decorating 18th century stays. This pair appears to have an embroidered design.

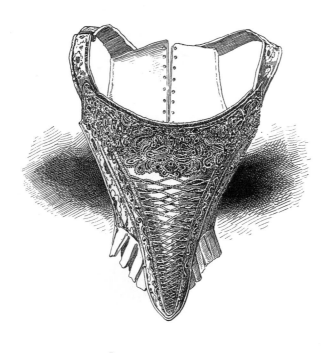

Brocade stays.

A typical 18th century corset.

Elaborate 18th century corsets.

Inside an 18th century corset-maker's shop.

The back view of a French corset from 1810.

A front view of the same corset. Notice how the emphasis is on flattening the figure for high-waisted, slim clothes.

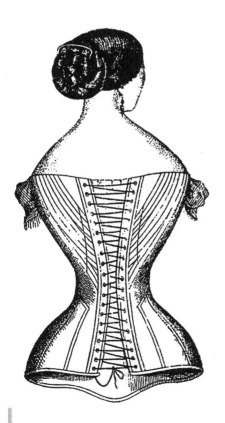

An 1845 corset laced up the rear.

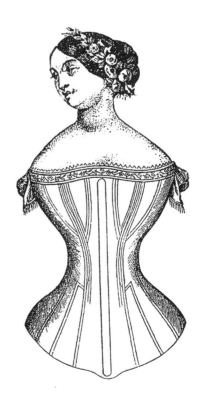

A front view of the same corset. Where most of the double lines are, whalebone was slipped inside the corset.

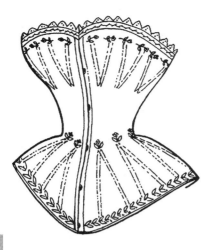

By the time this 1837 corset was made, the classic Victorian hourglass look was in vogue.

An 1851 illustration of Madame Caplin's petticoat suspending corset.

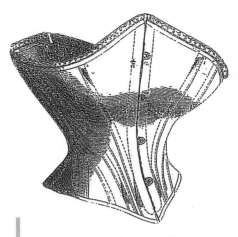

A short corset from 1863. Notice that steel clasps down the front—making getting in and out of the corset so much easier—were now standard.

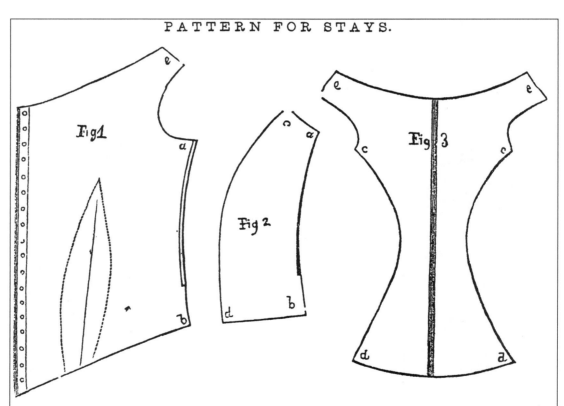

PATTERN FOR STAYS.

A CORRESPONDENT who has kindly furnished the above pattern writes respecting it as follows :—

"I have inclosed a pattern of a pair of stays, that I have worn for some time past, and can answer for their ease and convenience. I had suffered severely from a pain in my side, but since I have worn stays similar to this pattern, I have been much better. One yard and a quarter of satteen is sufficient to make them; and three lengths of whalebone, one on each side of the front, and another down the middle of the back, should be used. Hooks and eyelet-holes, or buttons, for fastenings."

Fig. 1. Front.   Fig. 2. Side-piece.
Fig. 3. The whole of the back.

In 1853, *Godey's Magazine and Lady's Book* ran this simple pattern for a corset.

PRACTICAL INSTRUCTIONS IN STAY MAKING.

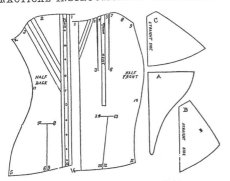

Materials necessary for making a Pair of Stays.—
Half a yard of material; a piece of stay-tape for casing;
some whalebone, either ready prepared, or in strips to be
split and shaved to size; a steel busk; wash-leather sufficient to cover it, and webbing to case it; a paper of 8-be-
tween needles; a reel of 25-cotton; a box of French holes;
and a punch for putting them in.

DIRECTIONS FOR TAKING THE MEASURE.

Measure round the waist as tightly as possible, noticing the number of inches ; deduct
two as an allowance for the clothes. Next
take the measure of the bust by placing the
measure in the middle of the chest, at No. 1
(see engraving), and pass it over the bosom
to No. 8, not tightly, and no allowance here to
be made for the clothes.

Then, from No. 8, passing the measure
closely under the arm, to No. 1 of the back,
which is not to reach the middle of the back
by an inch and a half ; next place the measure
at the bottom of the busk, and pass round
stomach and hips, allowing about four inches
for clothes, and then take the length of the
busk.

*It must be remembered that stays ought NOT TO
MEET when they are laced on.*

It will be found to simplify the directions
very much if a form, similar to the following,
be first prepared, and the number of inches
written against each as the part is measured ;
and then no confusion can possibly take place
in the cutting out:—

Waist
Bust
Back
Hips
Length of Busk.

DIRECTIONS FOR CUTTING OUT.

A pattern must now be prepared according
to the directions given in the engraving, which
can easily be done by enlarging the design,
and adding the requisite number of inches
between each figure.

THE BACK.—Double the material sufficiently
wide to take two whalebones, the holes, and
to turn-in for felling-down, as marked in the
engraving ; then lay on the pattern, and cut
out the two parts of the back together, allowing, for turnings-in, about half an inch at the
seam under the arm.

THE FRONT is cut out by placing the pattern
so that the straight way comes in the direction of the little bones up the bosom, leaving
a good turning-in up the front seam, which
crease off in pattern on the double material, as
it is better to cut out every part in the double,
that you may have each side exactly alike.

Should you desire to increase the size of
the stays, it must ALWAYS be done by allowing
the required additional size on the front and
back at the seam under the arm, and by pro-
portioning the armhole to the increased size.

When the bosom gores are to be put in, the
material is merely cut from No. 2 to No. 3,
and from No. 5 to No. 6, in a direct line, *cutting none away.* In cutting places for stomach
and hip-gores, in front and back, cut straight
up, and then from No. 7 to No. 8 in back, and
from No. 13 to No. 14 in front. Then cut out
all the gores, as directed in the engraving.

DIRECTIONS FOR MAKING.

1st.—Stitch a place for the first bone at
back, and for the holes, the width of half an
inch, keeping the line perfectly even, and fell
down a place for the second bone on the wrong
side.

2d.—Fit the bosom-gores by making a narrow turning-in from No. 2 to No. 3, and from
No. 3 to No. 4 ; fix the gore at 3, the straight
side of the gore next the busk, tacking it very
closely up to No. 2 ; then fix the other gore in
like manner at No. 6, the straight side next
the armhole, tacking up to No. 7.

3d.—With a measure, make the required
size across the bust, by increasing or diminish-
ing the gores at the top ; tack the other sides
very firmly from No. 3 to No. 4, and from No.
6 to No. 5, shaping them prettily, narrow at
the bottom, and of a rounded form towards
the top ; then stitch them very neatly ; and,
cutting away superfluous stuff on the wrong
side, hem down, beginning each side from No.
3 to No. 6.

4th.—Hem a piece of stay-tape at the back,
for little bones, and stitch down the middle of
it on the right side.

*The other half front to be done in a similar
manner.*

5th.—Put in the stomach-gores, turning in
from 14 to 15, and tacking the straight side
of the gore under it ; and fix the hip-gores in
the back in like manner, the straight side to
the holes.

6th.—Join the seams under the arm by pin-
ning No. 10 of half-front to No. 11 of half-
back, to half the size of waist required,
wrapping the front on to the back. Everywhere face each piece to its fellow piece, and
crease it, that it may be exactly the same
size and shape. Then do the other half in
the same way.

7th.—Having closed the seam, finish the
stomach and hip-gore by measuring and making to the size required round the hip, by let-
ting out or taking in, rounding them to fit the
hip ; face and crease the gores for the other
half, which is to be finished in the same
manner.

8th.—Take a piece of webbing wide enough
to case the busk when covered with wash-
leather ; double it exactly, and tack down the
half-front, the double edge being scrupulously
down the centre of the stays ; fell it on very
closely ; then stitch the two halves together
at the crease down the middle ; turn the other
half of the webbing on to the unfinished side,
and fell it down as before, turning in a little
piece top and bottom.

9th.—Bind the stays very neatly, top and
bottom.

10th.—Put in the holes, two near each other
at the top of the right side, and two near each
other at the bottom of the left side—the rest
at equal distances.

Proceed now to the boning, which do by
scraping them to fit nicely ; then, having
covered them with a piece of glazed calico,
cut, at the bottom of each bone place, a hole,
like a button-hole, and work it round like
one ; put the bones in, and drill a hole through
the stays and the bone, about an inch and a
half from the top and bottom of each bone,
and fasten them in with silk by bringing the
needle through the hole to the right side, and
passing it over the top of the bone, as marked
at No. 12. Then put in the busk ; and, if a
hook is required at the bottom, put that in
before the busk, which is best done by leaving
a short hole in the seam, and passing the hook
through, fastening it securely at the back.
The busk must be stitched in very firmly, top
and bottom.

Should the stays have become soiled in the
process of making, they are easily cleaned
with bread inside and out, and, when cleaned,
must be nicely pressed, taking care to make
no creases anywhere.

If these simple directions be strictly adhered
to in the making up, a pair of well-fitting
stays, at a trifling cost, will reward the pains
of the worker.

Although it was
rare for women
to make their own
corsets, or even
for seamstresses
to attempt them,
*Godey's Lady's
Book* ran these
instructions in 1857.

Douglas & Sherwood's Celebrated
Tournure Corset, patented in 1859.
The idea here was to replace the
hoop skirt with a corset that held
the skirts out. Unfortunately, layers
of petticoats would still be needed,
so the Tournure Corset never
caught on.

A back view of the Tournure Corset.

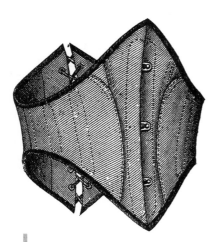

Young girl's corset.

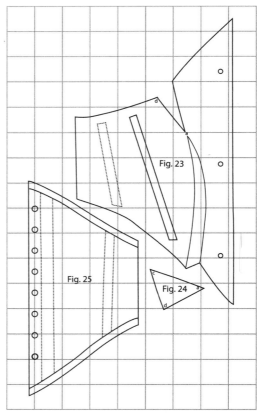

Scaled pattern for the same corset,
redrawn for the modern sewer.

1 square = 1''

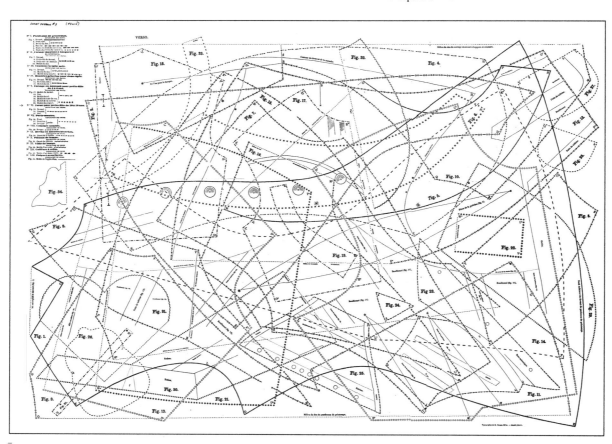

Pattern as presented in the February 4, 1866 issue of *La Mode Illustree*.

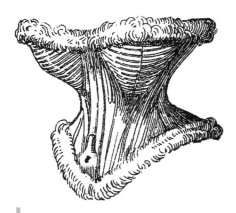

An elaborate, atypical corset from 1867.

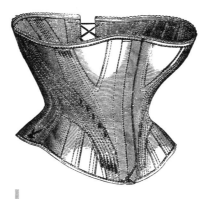

A nursing corset from 1869.

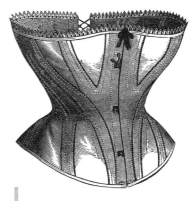

A corset from an 1869 issue of *Harper's Bazar*.

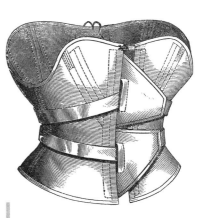

A corset made of complicated straps, pictured in an 1869 issue of *Harper's Bazar*.

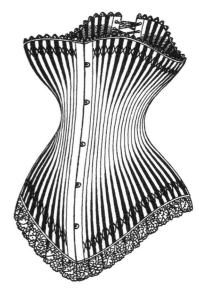

How Caplin represented a typical woman in a 1864 corset. An editor from *Peterson's Magazine* wrote in the same year: "The long, ungainly corset, as unbending as a coat of armor, and filled with whalebone and steel, oppressing the chest and keeping the body in close and painful imprisonment, has now been discarded, much to the benefit of the health and comfort of ladies...No French lady would think of wearing the old 'instrument of torture,' as it is now called." Manufacturers and fashion magazine editors all agreed that the new corsets were more comfortable.

Corsets of the mid to late 1870s were long. They featured lacing up the back and metal hooks in the front.

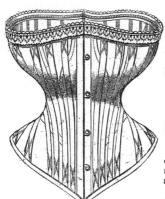
Thomson's corsets were widely advertised from second half of the 19th century through the early 20th century. This ad appeared in an 1871 issue of the *Metropolitan*.

Globe advertised this 1873 corset as made of "Naumkeag Satteen Jean, twenty bones, in white and colored, trimmed and embroidered" for $1, or "London Cord and French Coutille, and of very fine material, twenty bones, very handsomely trimmed and embroidered," $1.50 to $2.

A black sateen corset featured in an 1882 issue of *Harper's Bazar*.

A Thomson's corset from 1882.

One hundred bones and a woven, one-piece cloth were what made 1882's double hip corset unique.

Good Sense corsets were supposedly healthier than the standard, heavily boned corset. This corset was advertised in an 1886 issue of *Ladies' Home Journal*.

Dr. Scott's made corsets of every type, including nursing corsets and corset devices designed for flattening stomachs. This ad was featured in an 1886 *E. Butterick & Co.'s Catalogue*.

The Flynt Waist or True Corset

Is universally indorsed by eminent physicians as the
most SCIENTIFIC WAIST or CORSET known.
Pat. Jan. 6, 1874.

No. 1 represents a high-necked garment. No. 2, a low
necked one, which admits of being high in the back and
low front. No. 3 is to illustrate our mode of adjusting
the "Flynt Hose Support" each side of the hip, also, the
most correct way to apply the waistbands for the
drawers, under and outside petticoats and dress skirt.
No. 4 shows the Flynt Extension and Nursing Waist, appreciated by mothers. No. 5, the Misses' Waist, with
Hose Supports attached. No. 6, how we dress very little people. No, 7 illustrates how the warp threads of the
fabric cross at right angles in the back, thereby insuring in every waist, THE MOST SUCCESSFUL SHOULDER-
BRACE EVER CONSTRUCTED.
☞ Our "Manual," containing 46 pages of reading
matter, relating to the subject of Hygienic Modes of
Underdressing, sent free to any physician or lady, on
application to MRS. O. P. FLYNT, 319 Columbus ave.,
Boston, Mass. Columbus ave. cars pass all Depots.

The 1886 Flynt Waist was designed
to shape the figure more gently,
while at the same time reducing
backaches that tightly cinched
corsets often caused.

WARNER BRO'S

CELEBRATED
CORALINE
CORSETS

FLEXIBLE HIP ● NURSING
HEALTH ● ABDOMINAL ● CORALINE

Avoid cheap imitations made of various kinds
of cord. None are genuine unless
"DR. WARNER'S CORALINE"
is printed on inside of steel cover.

FOR SALE BY ALL LEADING MERCHANTS.

9, MILLION
worn during
the past six
years.

This marvel-
ous success is
due—

1st.—To the
superiority of
Coraline over
all other ma-
terials, as a
stiffener for
Corsets.

2d.—To the
superior qual-
ity, shape and
workmanship
of our Corsets,
combined with
their low
prices.

ELEGANT SHAPE,
HEALTH and
COMFORT
Perfectly Combined in
MADAME FOY'S
Skirt Supporting
CORSET.
It is one of the most
popular and satisfac-
tory in the market.
For sale by all lead-
ing dealers.
Price by mail $1.30.
FOY, HARMON &
CHADWICK, New Haven, Conn.

Madame Foy's corset, as seen
in an 1886 issue of *Ladies' Home
Journal*, was designed to take
some of the weight of the skirts
off a woman's waist through the
use of shoulder straps.

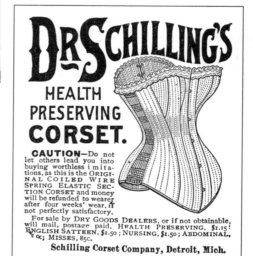

DrSchilling's

HEALTH
PRESERVING
CORSET.

CAUTION—Do not
let others lead you into
buying worthless imita-
tions, as this is the ORIGI-
NAL COILED WIRE
SPRING ELASTIC SEC-
TION CORSET and money
will be refunded to wearer
after four weeks' wear, if
not perfectly satisfactory.
For sale by DRY GOODS DEALERS, or if not obtainable,
will mail, postage paid, HEALTH PRESERVING, $1.15;
ENGLISH SATTEEN, $1.50; NURSING, $1.50; ABDOMINAL,
* 0c; MISSES, 85c.
Schilling Corset Company, Detroit, Mich.

Dr. Schilling's 1887 corset contained
some of the first stays made of
coiled steel. This made the corset
more flexible than those made with
ordinary whalebone or steel stays.

Stressing their "flexible hip" corsets, Warner
was a ready-made corset leader from the
1880s through the early 1900s. This corset was
advertised in *Ladies' Home Journal* in 1887.

EIGHT
Excellent reasons why every Lady should wear

BALL'S
HEALTH PRESERVING

CORSETS

1st. They need no breaking in.
2d. INVALIDS can wear them with ease
and Comfort, as they yield to every movement
of the body.
3d. They do not compress the most vital
parts of the wearer.
4th. They will fit a greater variety of forms
than any other make.
5th. Owing to their peculiar construction
they will last TWICE AS LONG as an ordinary
Corset.
6th. They have had the unqualified endorse-
ment of every Physician who has examined
them.
7th. They have given universal satisfaction
to all ladies who have worn them, the common
remark being,

"WE WILL NEVER WEAR ANY OTHER MAKE."

8th. They are the only Corset that the wearer
is allowed three weeks trial, and if not found
perfectly satisfactory in every respect the money is refunded.

FOR SALE BY
ALL LEADING DRY GOODS DEALERS.

CHICAGO CORSET CO.,
240 & 242 Monroe St., Chicago, Ill.
NEW YORK SALESROOM,
13 Lispenard Street.

Supposedly recommended
by doctors—even for invalid
women—the Ball corset
did not "compress the most
vital parts of the wearer." As
seen in the May 1886 issue of
Ladies' Home Journal.

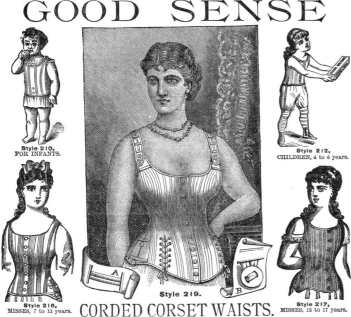

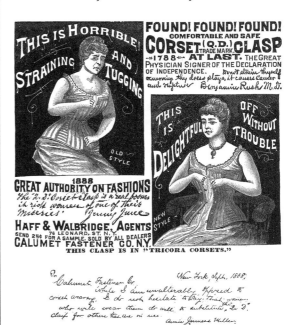

A more comfortable corset, as advertised in *Dress* magazine in 1888.

Ferris sold primarily corded corsets for infants, girls, and women. Their ads nearly always emphasized good health. This full-page ad was featured in an 1887 issue of the dress reform magazine *Dress*.

Advertised in an 1887 issue of *Dress*, Bates' Waist was a long, snug-fitting, but less rigid version of the corset. It was supposedly worn by many notable suffragettes and famous female authors.

An 1888 ad for a corset designed to give lady-like posture.

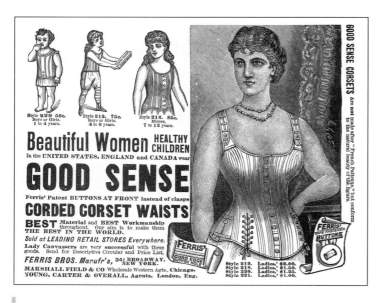

Good Sense corsets and waists replaced heavy whalebone or steel with cording. As seen in an 1888 issue of *Dress*.

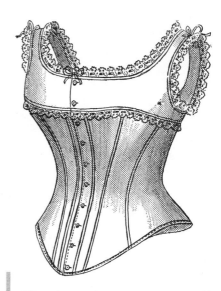

The alternative corset espoused by Annie Jenness Miller in the 1888 issue of *Dress*. Although featuring whalebone, these corsets were designed to be lightly—not tightly—cinched.

From agony to ease, that is what J. G. Fitzpatrick corsets promised in this 1889 ad.

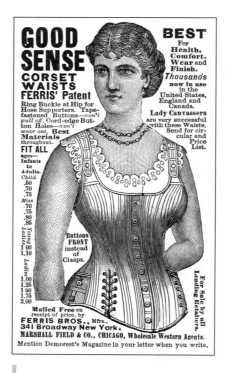

Corsets—especially ready-made corsets, like this one from 1889—were forever advertised as unbreakable. When tightly laced, many whalebone or featherbone corsets did break at the waist.

Although most Victorian corsets fastened with metal clasps in the front, which made getting in and out of the undergarment much easier, that long line of metal down the center did make movement—especially bending over—difficult. That's why so many "health" corsets, like this one, from an 1889 *Demorest's* magazine, featured buttons instead.

German image showing a woman in her undergarments.

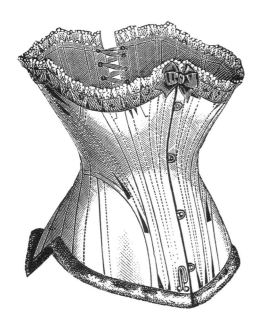

This corset, from *Harper's Bazar*, features special panels to encourage generous hips.

A German Hansen corset ad showcasing a corset-created, tiny waist.

What the average Victorian woman looked like in a corset. Large hips, stomach, and bosoms were encouraged.

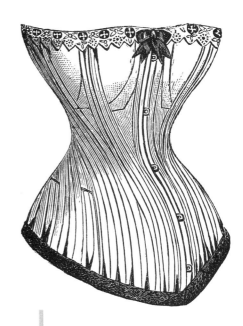

A satin corset from the 1880s.

3285
Front View.

3285
Back View.

Home seamstress corset patterns were extremely rare. Most women either purchased custom-made corsets from professional corset makers or they bought ready-made corsets. However, this corset must have been considered easy enough for any woman to sew. It was designed for wearing under a bathing suit, and was described the June 1890 issue of *The Delineator* as made from drilling, coutille, jean, or heavy muslin, with whalebones or steels.

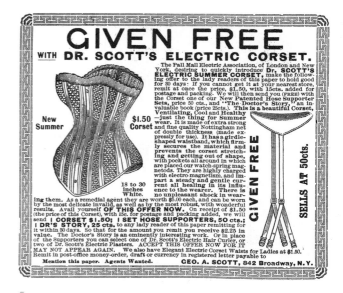

Dr. Scott's Electric Corset, as advertised in 1890, was $1.50 and came with free hose supporters.

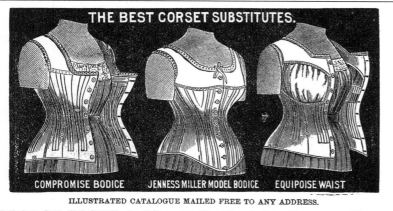

Annie Jenness Miller, one of the best-known proponents of women's dress reform, leant her name to these lightly boned corsets sold by George Frost & Co., as seen in the 1890 issue of *The Delineator*.

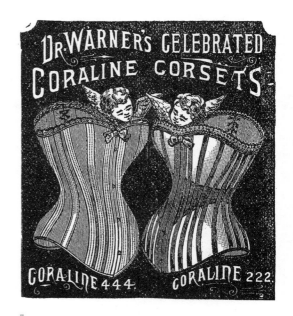

Supposedly fashioned after French corsets, but boned with Coraline, these corsets were advertised in 1890.

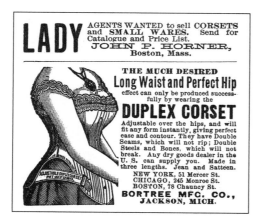

An interesting 1890 corset that makes room for voluptuous hips with a high cut and a hip band.

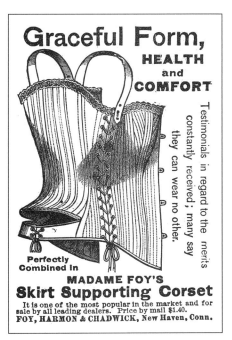

Graceful Form,
HEALTH and COMFORT

Testimonials in regard to the merits constantly received; many say they can wear no other.

Perfectly Combined in
MADAME FOY'S
Skirt Supporting Corset

It is one of the most popular in the market and for sale by all leading dealers. Price by mail $1.40.
FOY, HARMON & CHADWICK, New Haven, Conn.

During the late 19th century, there was much talk about how unhealthy is was for women to wear layers of heavy skirts supported only at the waist. In an attempt to address this concern, some corsets, like this one from 1890, were made with shoulder straps and were advertised as "skirt supporting."

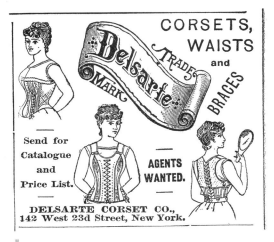

CORSETS, WAISTS and BRACES

Delsarte TRADE MARK

Send for Catalogue and Price List.

AGENTS WANTED.

DELSARTE CORSET CO.,
142 West 23d Street, New York.

Corsets were fully boned with whalebone, feather boning, or steel bands, and laced up the back. Waists were lighter corsets, containing either fewer bones or stiffened with cording. Braces were designed to reduce backaches, so common with tight lacing, or correct poor posture. From the May 1891 issue of *The Delineator*.

FERRIS' GOOD SENSE
Corset Waists

AVOID IMITATIONS.

Made to fit all Shapes and Sizes.

Send for Illus. Circular

BEST SHAPE.

MATERIAL. Workmanship.
Tape-fastened Buttons. Cord-edge Button Holes. Ring Buckle at hip. Permit full expansion of lungs. Support Skirts and Stockings. Gives satisfaction. Be sure your Waist is stamped "GOOD SENSE."
FERRIS BROS. Manufacturers and Patentees, 341 Broadway, New York
MARSHALL FIELD & CO., CHICAGO, Wholesale Western Agts.
For Sale by ALL LEADING RETAILERS.

Ferris corsets are for young girls, as seen in an 1891 issue of *Ladies' Home Journal*.

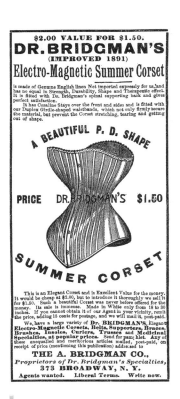

$2.00 VALUE FOR $1.50.
DR. BRIDGMAN'S
(IMPROVED 1891)
Electro-Magnetic Summer Corset

is made of Genuine English linen Net imported expressly for us, and has no equal in Strength, Durability, Shape and Therapeutic effect. It is fitted with Dr. Bridgman's spinal supporting back and gives perfect satisfaction.
It has Coraline Stays over the front and sides and is fitted with our Duplex Girdle-shaped waistbands, which not only firmly secure the material, but prevent the Corset stretching, tearing and getting out of shape.

A BEAUTIFUL P. D. SHAPE

PRICE DR. BRIDGMAN'S $1.50

SUMMER CORSET

This is an Elegant Corset and is Excellent Value for the money. It would be cheap at $2.00, but to introduce it thoroughly we sell it for $1.50. Such a beautiful Corset was never before offered for the money. Its sale is immense. Made in White only from 18 to 30 inches. If you cannot obtain it of our Agent in your vicinity, remit the price, adding 15 cents for postage, and we will mail it, post-paid.
We have a large variety of Dr. BRIDGMAN'S Elegant Electro-Magnetic Corsets, Belts, Supporters, Braces, Brushes, Insoles, Curlers, Trusses and Medicinal Specialties, at popular prices. Send for pamphlet. Any of these unequalled and meritorious articles mailed, post-paid, on receipt of price (mentioning this publication) addressed to
THE A. BRIDGMAN CO.,
Proprietors of Dr. Bridgman's Specialties,
373 BROADWAY, N. Y.
Agents wanted. Liberal Terms. Write now.

In the 1890s, "electric" was a hot word used to sell everything from corsets to health products. This electric corset was advertised in 1891.

BLACK CORSETS.

LANGDON & BATCHELLER'S GENUINE THOMSON'S GLOVE FITTING

The utmost perfection in the art of Corset Making has been reached in our STYLE B CORSET cut on the latest French designs, in SHORT, MEDIUM and EXTRA LONG waists.

These Corsets will satisfy the most fastidious.

MADE IN ROYAL FAST BLACK, WHITE AND FRENCH GRAY.

"The utmost perfection in the art of Corset Making has been reached in our Style B Corset cut on the latest French designs, in short, medium and extra long waists," said a Thomson's Glove Fitting Corset ad from 1891. "These corsets will satisfy the most fastidious."

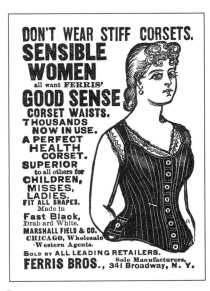

DON'T WEAR STIFF CORSETS.
SENSIBLE WOMEN
all want FERRIS'
GOOD SENSE
CORSET WAISTS.
THOUSANDS NOW IN USE.
A PERFECT HEALTH CORSET.
SUPERIOR to all others for **CHILDREN, MISSES, LADIES.**
FIT ALL SHAPES.
Made in **Fast Black,** Drab and White.
MARSHALL FIELD & CO. CHICAGO, Wholesale Western Agents.
SOLD BY ALL LEADING RETAILERS.
FERRIS BROS., Sole Manufacturers, 341 Broadway, N. Y.

Good Sense corsets, like these from 1891, appealed to active women or those who believed traditional corsets were dangerous to a woman's health. They were lightly boned and featured buttons down the front instead of stiff metal clasps.

Interesting to Ladies.

The beauty of woman is in the sense of her clothes. It is true that clothes do not make the woman, yet they help the appearance of the woman. Sensible dressing is always artistic and throws into relief the modest beauty of the figure. The fashionably modeled corset cannot make the figure fashionable unless the figure be naturally so modeled. The corset may cover ill shape beneath, and give apparent graceful curves and lines, but a pinched-up waist and an artificial bust are neither natural nor artistic, and the woman who so attempts to build outside appearance is reckoned for what she is, frequently for worse than she is. She does not even deceive herself. The Equipoise Waist has been worn by intelligent women for fourteen years. No other corset substitute has ever given such universal satisfaction. It is recommended by sensible women everywhere and by the leading physicians at home and abroad. It fully embodies the true hygienic principle of support from the shoulders. The perfect modeling and careful adjustment of each part with relation to the others so equally distributes the strain and pull of the garments attached that their weight is hardly perceptible. The bone pockets are so constructed that the bones can be removed without ripping. The ready-made Equipoise Waist fits the wearer as though especially made to her measure.

The materials used in its construction are of the best procurable quality. *The Equipoise Waist is guaranteed to wear twice as long as any other waist or corset, irrespective of cost.* Made by George Frost Co., 31 Bedford Street, Boston, Mass. Send Stamp for a copy of our finely illustrated book on sensible dressing, which contains a list of merchants who sell the Equipoise Waist.

If they are not sold in your city or town you can order from us by mail without extra expense.

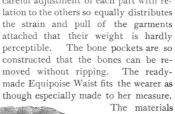

Equipoise Waist.

**GEO. FROST COMPANY,
Boston, Mass.**

A pinched up waist and artificial bust are neither natural nor artistic" opined an 1892 ad for Geo. Frost Company's Equipoise Waist. Naturally, their own corset was different, being worn by "intelligent women for fourteen years." The corset featured wide shoulder bands and easy-to-remove boning.

Corsets that covered the bust were called "corset and waist in one." This one was advertised in 1892.

Ready made corsets were often placed on mannequins and steamed to shrink them to a desirable shape. L. L. Loomer's Sons 1892 corsets were made this way and were, according to the maker, "the best in the world."

Madame Griswold's Patent Skirt-Supporting Corset from 1892 was considered more healthy because the shoulder straps helped carry the weight of the skirts on the shoulders, not just the waist. It also featured "springs" instead of bones.

Once well-laced, corsets were difficult to remove—unless they featured metal clasps running down the front. This 1892 ad showcases the "magic corset clasp," a style of clasp that was fairly standard.

An 1893 corset with a back brace.

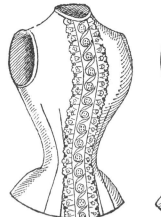 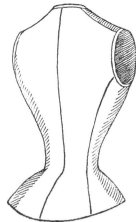

A "corset waist," described as "made of cautille or drilling, and meets the demand for a comfortable and supporting waist to be worn in place of a corset. Whalebones can be inserted in the front, sides and back, and the backs are cut with shoulder straps that button to the fronts." As featured in the Winter 1892–93 issue of *Domestic Fashion Review*.

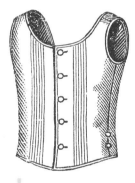 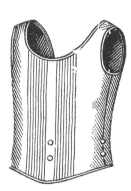

An 1892 child's corset waist, "usually made of cautille, jean or muslin." It was corded for stiffness.

The Jackson Corset Waist from 1893 promised comfort, health, grace, and economy.

Take your Exercises
IN A
Delsarte Girdle
OR A
Delsarte Waist

BOTH ARE PERFECTION

Girdle with Empire Gowns

Send for illustrated price list

DELSARTE CORSET CO.
124 W. 23d St., N. Y.
111 State St., Chicago, Ill.

As sports and gymnasium exercise became more popular for women in the late 19th century, corsets allowing freedom of movement became necessary. The Delsarte Girdle or Waist, advertised here in 1893, promised to make exercise much easier.

"Adequate support" with "grace of person" is what the makers of this 1893 Jackson Favorite Waist promised.

This Kosmo corset from 1893, made from French sateen and trimmed with embroidery, would outwear six ordinary corsets, claimed the manufacturer.

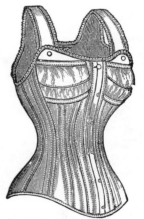
The Grand Rapids Corset Waist, as advertised in the March 1893 issue of *The Delineator*, featured buttoned straps and a slightly puffed bosom.

Feather boning was a relatively new corset offering in the 1890s, giving corsets a bit more flexibility than traditional whalebone or steel stays. This corset was advertised in an 1893 issue of *The Delineator*.

Women in corsets could not bend over completely at the waist, so when gymnastics for women became popular, corded "waists," like this one from 1893, were worn for "taking exercise."

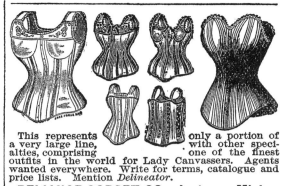

From infancy through womanhood, Reliance offered an appropriate corset. As featured in the June 1893 issue of *The Delineator*.

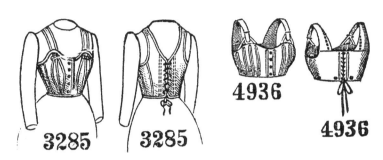

Sewing patterns for corsets were extremely rare, but in 1893, leading pattern company manufacturer Butterick offered these two designs. One, designed for swimming, and another in the "Empire" style. It's likely both were stiffened with cording instead of boning or steel.

An 1893 "empire" corset of longer length, reaching just a bit below the hips. Most so-called empire corsets ended at the rib cage

Mrs. Frank Leslie says, "I have found them of **great** use in preventing the breaking of Corset bones, **and** also in keeping them in shape."

PEARL CORSET SHIELDS

WITHOUT STEELS OR BONES

THREE SIZES

SOLD BY YOUR DEALER

THEY DO **NOT** ENLARGE THE WAIST

PREVENT CORSETS BREAKING

REPAIR BROKEN ONES.

All Dry Goods Stores sell Pearl Corset Shields; sample pair, 25 cts. prepaid.
EUGENE PEARL, 23 Union Square, W., New York.

Ferris' Good Sense Waist

Best for Health, Economy and Beauty.
BUTTONS at front instead of CLASPS.
RING BUCKLE at hip for Hose supporters.
Tape-fastened Buttons—*won't pull off.*
Cord - Edge Button Holes—*won't wear out.*
FIT ALL AGES—
Infants to Adults.
For Sale by All
Leading Retailers.
MARSHALL FIELD & CO.
West'n Wholesale Depot.
Send for illus.
circular to FERRIS BROS., Manuf'rs.
Principal Office—341 Broadway, New York.
Branch Office—18 Sutter Street, San Francisco, Cal.

The Snug-Fitting, Beautifully Made Jackson Favorite Waist.

Mrs. A. E. WHITAKER, of Boston, writes in substance of the JACKSON FAVORITE WAIST: A health waist that **gives the support** of a corset without unduly compressing the waist and other organs, and, as compared with other improved garments, inexpensive. Women, while they wish to dress and look neatly, sometimes find it impossible to wear corsets while at work and are obliged to discard them a part of the time. This is not wise or healthful. A **good, firm waist,** with shoulder-straps to help hold up the weight of the clothes, is much better. I have examined all the different waists manufactured and given them a trial as to fit and wearing qualities, and can recommend the Jackson Favorite Waist as comfortable, well-fitting, fulfilling the needed requirements at **half the cost** of the best improved waists.

Ladies frequently order **two and sometimes three** of these Waists at one time, an expression of satisfaction rarely accorded goods of this class. Mrs. J., Los Angeles, Cal., says: "Your Waist is just what I have been watching for: I wish two of size 23." Miss A., Delta, Cal.: "I will not wear any other waist as long as I can procure the Jackson Favorite." Miss McD., of Redfield, Me.: "Waist reached me all right; am delighted with it." Miss P., Pittsfield, Pa.: "Waist received to-day and gives perfect satisfaction. Enclosed find postal-note for another." Mrs. M., Boston Highlands: "Send two more of the Jackson Favorite Waists, sizes 21 and 22 in black. I received mine this morning and was so pleased with it that two friends each wanted one." Miss E., Kenneth, Pa.: "Your waists are **superior in finish** to any I have yet seen. I enclose $1 for another."

600,000 Ladies and Misses wear the Jackson Favorite Waist.

Women who tightly cinched their waists sometimes had trouble with their corset bones breaking. This 1893 Pearl Corset Shield ad promises to do away with that problem with small pads added to the corset that "do not enlarge the waist."

For those concerned about the health risks supposedly associated with traditional corseting, there was the Ferris' Good Sense corset. This one was advertised in 1893.

An 1893 corset designed for those who feared tight lacing was the cause of many ills.

Any Woman Will Say So.

It wouldn't make much difference what *we* said about Dr. Warner's corsets if there were not several hundred thousand women in **every part** of the community to confirm our statements with "That's so."

The Coraline we use is superior to whalebone and absolutely unbreakable.

What we want is to have you try Dr. Warner's corsets. You'll never wear any other kind.

We especially recommend Fanita, fine coutil, $3.00; Fine coutil, 888, sateen strips, $1.75; Fine sateen, embroidered, No. 777, at $1.50; Fine sateen, 444, at $1.35; and heavy jean, No. 333, sateen strips, at $1.10.

WARNER BROS.,
359 Broadway, New York.

BEAUTY ACCOMMODATION WAIST, No. 7, gives perfect form with ease of movement, develops bust, while not enlarging waist. Tampico Dress Forms with each Waist. Removable Steels, Adjustable Shoulder Straps, Laced at Back, Buttoned Front, Curved at Back to the Figure. In White and Black, 18 to 30 in. By mail, for **$1.50.** Little Beauty Waists for children, *the best.* Catalogue free.
E. H. HORWOOD & CO., 51 MERCER ST., N.Y.

Warner corsets were the first corsets heavily advertised as having coraline boning. As seen in the March 1893 issue of *The Delineator.*

For women who wanted a more ample bosom, but not wider hips, there was the "Accommodation Waist," advertised in 1893.

As fashions gradually decreed a longer waist, many women had to rely on corsets to produce the look. This corset was highlighted in an 1897 ad.

The makers of the 1897 Chicago Waist claimed their corset was the most popular in America.

Just like today, patriotism was used to sell products—even corsets. This ad appeared in the November 1897 issue of *The Delineator*.

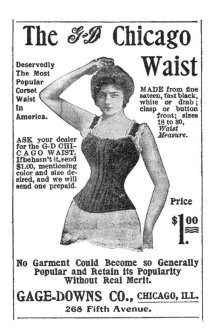

"The most popular corset waist in America," this 1898 Chicago Waist ad proclaimed, costing just $1.

Oddly showing Mary, Queen of Scots in a late 19th century corset, this ad promises that while "every woman cannot have such a beautiful face as Mary, 'Queen of Scots'… every woman can have a graceful form by wearing Kabo Corsets."

This 1899 Cresco corset had an innovative design. It was essentially a short corset, ending at the waist, attached loosely to the bottom half of a long corset that controlled the hips and stomach.

There's one Corset you won't have to "break in." One that will fit perfectly and gives thorough satisfaction.

The *American Lady* French Gored Corset

Style 352, for $1.00.

The latest creation in the Corset Art. Made in Short and Long Waist, White and Drab....

SCHILLING CORSET CO.,

Mfrs., Detroit, Mich.

NEW YORK—65 AND 67 WOOSTER STREET, CHICAGO—234 AND 236 FRANKLIN STREET.

SENT PREPAID ON RECEIPT OF PRICE, IF YOUR DEALER DOES NOT SELL THEM.

The average corset price at this time, as seen in fashion ads, was $1. This ad appeared in an 1897 issue of *The Delineator.*

THE DOWAGER CORSET

Is the Best Corset Produced

FOR STOUT FIGURES.

Made in three lengths—Extra Long, Long and Medium. Sizes 22 to 43 ins.
Style 550, Heavy Coutil, Satteen strips. Sizes 22 to 30, $2.00; 31 to 36, $2.25; 37 to 43, $2.50. White, Drab and Black.
Style 550, Summer Netting (white only). Sizes and prices same as above.
Style 614, Fine Sateen, Italian finish. Sizes 22 to 30, $3.50; 31 to 36, $3.75; 37 to 43, $4.00. White, Drab and Black.

The following Testimonials are taken from thousands of similar nature:

"I have succeeded in getting a corset of your 550 model, 'The Dowager.' It is the most comfortable corset I have ever had."

"I have tried every known make in unbreakable corsets. Have worn 'The Dowager' for three years past, and recommend it to all my friends."

"I wear a 'Royal Worcester Corset,' Style 550, and for comfort, shapeliness and durability, prefer it to the $6.50 corset made to order that I have worn."

ROYAL WORCESTER CORSETS

AND

THE DOWAGER CORSET

Are sold by dealers everywhere. Ask your dealer FIRST. If he can't supply you, a money order sent us, with size, length and color plainly specified, will bring corset to you free of expense.

Send for Illustrated Catalogue

THE DOWAGER CORSET

WORCESTER CORSET COMPANY,

WORCESTER, MASS.   CHICAGO, ILL.

For women past their youth and with "stout" figures, the 1899 Dowager Corset promised to come to the rescue.

Wear MARTHA WASHINGTON WAISTS FOR HEALTH AND COMFORT.

Good sense is displayed in the manufacture of these garments in every detail. Made of best materials, most skilful workmanship, perfect in all their lines without injurious pressure. Far superior to any other waist on the market. If not for sale at your dealer's, we will send you a pair, mailing free, upon receipt of the following prices:

Martha Washington Ladies' . . . . . One Dollar
Martha Washington Young Ladies' . . . 75 Cents
Martha Washington Misses' . . . . . . 50 Cents
Martha Washington Children's . . . . . 25 Cents

SEND WAIST MEASURE IN ORDERING.

BIRDSEY, SOMERS & CO., 349 Broadway, New York.

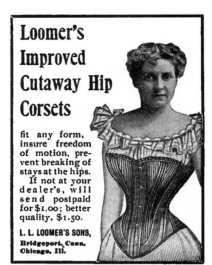

Loomer's Improved Cutaway Hip Corsets

fit any form, insure freedom of motion, prevent breaking of stays at the hips.

If not at your dealer's, will send postpaid for $1.00; better quality, $1.50.

L. L. LOOMER'S SONS,
Bridgeport, Conn.
Chicago, Ill.

Long corsets were problematic because they made movement difficult. This Loomer's corset, advertised in the May 1899 issue of *The Delineator*, had elastic along the hips and promised to make movement easier.

A Wonderful Corset!

ARMORSIDE

NEVER BREAKS

DOWN ON THE SIDES

CORSET

Positively the best value for $1.00 ever offered. The patented vertical boning makes it impossible to break at the sides. Made throughout of best materials, superior in many respects to corsets that you pay double this money for.

If not for sale at your dealer's, send $1.00 for a pair, mailage free, to

BIRDSEY, SOMERS & CO.,

439 Broadway,   NEW YORK.

The "patented vertical boning" on this corset ensured it would never "break at the sides," according to this 1899 ad.

Hearkening back to another age, Martha Washington corsets were nonetheless perfectly shaped for 1890s fashions. This ad appeared in the July 1899 issue of *The Delineator.*

A typical corset of 1899, selling for $1 to $1.50, depending upon the material used.

Some corsets featured judicious use of elastic—as this 1899 corset does along the bust line.

A nursing corset featured in _Century Magazine_.

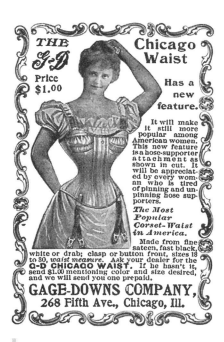

This 1899 "Chicago Waist" displays all the most popular corset features of the late 19th century: shoulder straps, elastic along the bust, and attached garters.

A trade card from the 1890s, showing a Dr. Warner's corset with coraline stiffening.

A stereograph photo with the caption: "Reducing the Surplus. 'Now, Pull Hard!'"

A trade card featuring the latest buzz word: "electric." Despite the name, no electricity was involved.

A postcard from the late 1890s or early 1900s.

A typical 1890s corset.

A Gibson Girl style corset featuring trim at the bust, to beautify and make the bosom larger.

The Imperial summer corset, made of mesh.

THOMSON'S
"Glove-Fitting"
CORSETS

are definitely superior in shape, wearing qualities and comfort. The seams **run around the body**. This is true of no other corset. They hold their shape permanently and give perfect fit. Every corset stamped with our name.

Turn them over and see how they're made.

This is a picture of

OUR VENTILATING CORSET

(Trade-Mark Registered), made of imported netting, stripped with coutil, and trimmed with lace and baby ribbon. **$1.00** a pair at all dealers. Light as a feather, yet strong as the strongest.

Handsome illustrated catalogue mailed *free*.

GEO. C. BATCHELLER & CO., 345 Broadway, N.Y.

This 1900 Thompson's ad reveals the boning and the complexity of corsets of this era.

W. B. Erect Form CORSETS

THE "W. B. ERECT FORM" Corset gives a long, low and full effect from shoulder to bust. It is the only correct model for the new straight front costumes. It throws the shoulders back into a fine military pose. It inflicts no strain upon bust or abdomen, and thus does away with those faults of corset construction which often lead to indigestion, short breathing and sometimes even more serious trouble. THE "ERECT FORM" does not strain the figure—all the pressure of lacing is upon the hips and back muscles.

ERECT FORM Style 721, with 10-in. extra heavy boned steel. Of white and drab Jean. Hip gored **$1.00**

ERECT FORM Style 700, Hip gored. Of Imported Diamond Sateen in white and drab. **$1.50**

ERECT FORM Style 965, made of imported Coutil. Full gored bias cut. For small slender figures. **$1.75**

ERECT FORM Style 955, Improved, French **$2.00** Coutil in white and drab. Full gored bias cut.

ERECT FORM Style 955, made of Imported Coutil. Full gored bias cut. Heavily boned. For fully developed figures. Price **$2.50**

ERECT FORM Style 956, made of extra heavy French Coutil in white and rose, and of black Sateen. Full gored and bias cut. Price **$2.50**

These corsets are on sale in every part of the United States and Canada. If your dealer does not carry the corset you desire, send his name and amount, covering price of the model you want to our Dept. S, and we will forward the corset, prepaying all charges.

IMPORTANT.—In remitting send money order or registered letter for safety's sake.

A Little Book on **"How to Wear and Lace a Corset,"** will be mailed to anyone who sends for it.

W. B. Model 77.
A Short French Shape.

For slender and small women. Being extremely short it is made with boning instead of side steels. Has 11 in. 4 hook clasp. Extremely beautiful in contour. Fits snugly at waist and accentuates to the fullest extent bust and hips. Sizes 18 to 26. **$1.00**

W. B. Model 654.
A Popular French Shape.

It is the next most demanded corset after the "ERECT FORM" and is better suited for some figures. Model 654 has no side steels, which would inflict some discomfort in so short a corset, but is well stayed instead. Price **$1.00**

WEINGARTEN BROS.
Largest Corset Manufacturers in the World! 377 BROADWAY NEW YORK.

W. B.'s 1901 "Erect Form" corset with an elongated torso. "It throws the shoulders back into a fine military pose," the manufacturer claimed. "It inflicts no strain upon bust or abdomen, and this does away with those faults of corset construction which often lead to indigestion, short breathing and sometimes even more serious trouble."

FERRIS
GOOD SENSE WAIST

The unity of Health and Grace

The comfort of every movement is enhanced by the beautiful lines of the Ferris Waist. Whether on duty or on pleasure bent, the wearer is conscious of a unity of health and grace. It gives support without constraint.

Ferris Good Sense Corset Waists are made in all shapes and sizes to suit every form—with long or short waist, high or low bust. Sold by all leading retailers. Illustrated catalogue free. Finest material and workmanship.

THE FERRIS BROS. COMPANY, 341 Broadway, New York.

A Ferris Good Sense Waist ad, as featured in the March 1901 issue of *Modes and Fabrics*.

A short W. B. corset (Model 77) "for slender and small women," according to a 1901 ad. W. B. claimed this 1901 corset (Model 654) was the "next most demanded corset after the 'Erect Form,' and is better suited for some figures."

A long, lean corset from a 1902
Bon Marché catalog.

A corset featured in a 1902 French catalog.

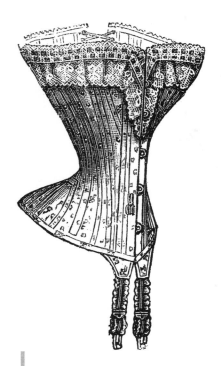

A 1902 corset with attached
suspenders for stockings.

A 1902 example of a child's corset. This one
is for a boy and was stiffened with cording to
encourage correct posture.

THE GREAT SUCCESS

F. P. Military Form

Style No. 852

THIS new creation has become the *most popular*, in a short time, of any corset ever produced in this country. It has all the attractive features that the best skill can produce. It is the *First Straight Front Corset* made in America, and is to-day by far the largest seller.

Made by a genuine French artist from Paris. *Made of the very best materials*, full French gore, bias cut, long hip, giving the *new and correct figure* to the wearer.

Has all the appearance of a much more expensive garment, and we will warrant it to *wear as well as corsets costing three times the price.*

Made in White and Drab. Every pair *warranted* to give satisfaction or money refunded.

Price $1.00 per pair

If not for sale at your dealer's, send us $1.00, and we will mail you a pair.

BIRDSEY & SOMERS
MANUFACTURERS
349 Broadway, New York

Claiming to be the first American corset to achieve the fashionable "straight front" look, 1902's F. P. Military Form promised to throw the hips back while moving the bust forward.

Is this what you need?

HENDERSON

ETON Girdle= Corset

Style 444

WHITE
DRAB
PINK
BLUE

Sizes 18 to 26

Price $1.00

It is the acme of perfection for slight and medium figures. It has the shape and effect of a Straight Front Corset and the ease and comfort of a Girdle.

AURORA CORSET CO.
Aurora, Illinois

For those who wanted only a little bit of fashionable shaping, the Eton Girdle-Corset, as advertised in the March 1902 issue of *The Delineator,* was a possibility.

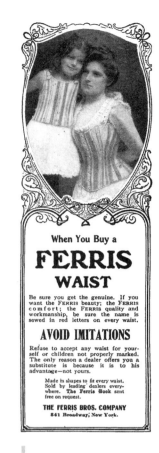

When You Buy a

FERRIS WAIST

Be sure you get the genuine. If you want the FERRIS beauty; the FERRIS comfort; the FERRIS quality and workmanship, be sure the name is sewed in red letters on every waist.

AVOID IMITATIONS

Refuse to accept any waist for yourself or children not properly marked. The only reason a dealer offers you a substitute is because it is to his advantage—not yours.

Made in shapes to fit every waist. Sold by leading dealers everywhere. The Ferris Book sent free on request.

THE FERRIS BROS. COMPANY
341 Broadway, New York.

Many girls wore "training corsets" like this 1902 Ferris waist.

THE EASY Z WAIST

Every mother of a growing boy or girl between the ages of two and twelve should know that the E-Z Waist is the only waist which yields in every direction and in every respect. The straps that strengthen it are as elastic as the rest of the waist. Buttons are sewed to these straps, which yield with every tug and pull and, therefore, the buttons do not come off.

Two styles of waists—one for boys and one for girls.

Booklet, "Room To Grow In," FREE to mothers of children.

Your dealer should keep the E-Z Waist. If not, send 25 cents for sample, giving age and stating whether the child is a boy or girl.

THE E-Z WAIST COMPANY, 102 Kingston Street, BOSTON, MASS.

Infants in the 19th century wore flannel waists— vest-like garments designed to keep them warm. But by the time a girl was about 4 years old, she wore a corset-like garment using cording instead of boning or steel stays like this E-Z Waist from 1902.

THOMSON'S "GLOVE-FITTING" "MILITANT"

VENTILATING

"The Queen of Summer Corsets"

Has held its own against all competition for the past thirty-five years. The only genuine "Ventilating" Corset in the newest straight-front style.

All the Leading Stores Sell Them

Artistic Catalogue mailed on request

Sole Manufacturers

GEO. C. BATCHELLER & CO.
345-347 Broadway, New York.

Sometimes summer corsets of this period, like this one featured in the July 1902 issue of *The Delineator,* were made from mesh-like fabric, designed to make the wearer cooler. Winter corsets were sometimes made of flannel or wool.

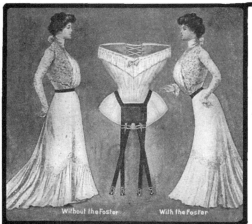

The Straight Military Front

shown in figure to right
is secured by wearing the

Foster Hose Supporter
Patented December 5, 1899.

The only supporter with a pad large enough and supporting bands strong enough to hold back the entire abdomen, assuring the wearer a correct standing position and the much desired straight front. It has a waist band which presses on the sides of the waist, making it round, and has no metal parts to mar or tear the corset.

THREE GRADES:

Wide web, black or white,	**60c.**
Wide web, fancy frilled, black, white, cardinal, blue or pink,	**75c.**
Heavy silk web, large pad if desired,	**$1.25**

The name "Foster" is stamped on every pair. Don't let your dealer impose on you with "*something just the same as 'The Foster.'*" If he hasn't it, we will mail it to you on receipt of price. Give color desired and your height and waist measure.

Without the Foster   *With the Foster*

THE FOSTER HOSE SUPPORTER CO. - 438 Broadway, New York

Because stockings were still two separate garments (one worn on each leg), stocking supporters, worn over the corset, were necessary. From a 1902 issue of *The Delineator*.

Perfect Form and Girdle Combined

White and Drab Satteen
Price, $1.20. Sizes, 18 to 26
Girdles, 95 cents.

AGENTS WANTED for the above and for our Custom-Made Corsets.

BARCLEY CORSETS give perfect figures. Special patented features. Sell on sight. Write for terms and price list.

Barcley Corset Co.
334 Mulberry St.
Newark, N. J.

Like many corset ads, this one from 1902 promises a "perfect form" to every wearer.

A Corset that Cannot Break at the Waist

It matters not what the style of a corset is or what it is made of, if it breaks at the waist line it is rendered uncomfortable and useless.

The Cresco Corset

is disconnected in front at the waist line, and has elastic gores at each side, so it *cannot break at the waist.* Suitable for any day and all the day. Good to work in, walk in or rest in. It is shapely, comfortable and durable, and as it cannot break at the waist it is the *Cheapest Corset a Lady can buy.*

Where the **Cresco** is not kept by dealers it will be sent postpaid, for $1. Drab or White, Long, Short or Medium length. The next time you buy a corset try the **Cresco.**

THE MICHIGAN CORSET CO.,   -   JACKSON, MICHIGAN

This 1902 Cresco ad claimed their product would never break at the waist, since their corsets featured elastic sections along the waistline.

THE GILBERT CREST CORSET

Insures the straight front effect, the flat abdomen, the gracefully rounded hips—in a word, that charm of figure which every woman desires. The upper section overlaps the under section, giving double bones and so double strength where most needed. When the body is bent in any direction, these sections give slightly on each other, which prevents the corset breaking at the waist line. All bones and steels absolutely rust proof.

Our New Catalogue is the most helpful, at the same time the most beautiful Corset Catalogue ever issued. Write for it—No Charge.

We Want as Agent An active woman in every town and city in the U. S. Liberal commissions and exclusive territory given. We assist our agents in every possible way. Write for particulars.

GILBERT MFG. COMPANY
70 Centre St., NEW HAVEN, CONN.

This 1902 ad proclaims, "The Gilbert Crest Corset insures the straight front effect, the flat abdomen, the gracefully rounded hips—in a word, that charm of figure which every woman desires."

Venus HOSE SUPPORTER

STAND ERECT

Abdomen in—the easy swing from the shoulders, straight front, narrow hipped appearance—Possible if you wear the **Venus Hose Supporter.** Gives a graceful carriage, long naturally tapering waist and the flat, unbroken line from the shoulder that is Fashion's latest demand. Designed for all figures. Sold by all dealers; if yours hasn't the "Venus," order from us.

Made in pale blue, pink, red, black and white frilled silk elastic satin band, ornamental metal parts and Flexo fasteners. Per pair . . . **50c.**

Send for our free booklet of garter and hose supporter novelties for men, women and children.

A. STEIN & CO.
261 Fifth Ave., Chicago

This Venus hose supporter ad shows how turn-of-the-century garters fit over the corset.

Taming hips, which naturally protruded with older-style corsets, became a chief selling point in the early 1900s.

This American Beauty ad claims to be "the favorite corset of millions of discriminating women."

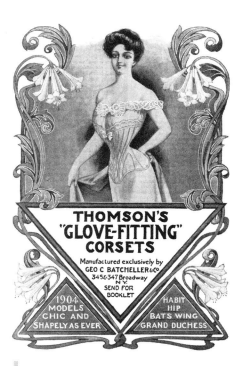

Thomson's Glove Fitting Corsets were some of the most popular at the turn of the century.

Kabo's ads often stressed the company's years in the business—in this case 24 years.

To moderns, the thought of putting
"babies, girls, and boys" in corsets
seems absurd. But well into the
20th century, this was a common
practice. Fortunately, corsets for
infants and young children were
not boned, but they did usually
have stiffening by means of stiff
cords sewn into the seams. A girl
might expect to switch to a boned
corset in her early teens.

Warner's was one of the most
popular makers of ready-made
corsets during the late 19th and
early 20th century.

Bragging about their recent grand prize from the St. Louis
World's Fair, this 1905 Kobo ad offers to send customers a
corset ribbon and special threading needle for just 2¢.

Tight corsets were considered right
corsets by the fashionable, and this
"Pinchin" 1905 corset ad promises to
pinch the waist so tight the corset will
not loosen or relax during wearing.

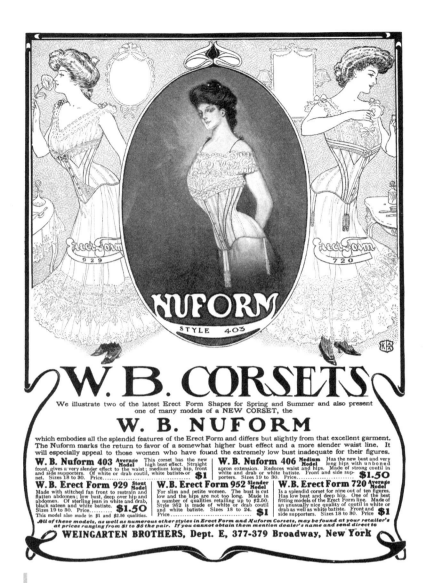

W. B. CORSETS

We illustrate two of the latest Erect Form Shapes for Spring and Summer and also present one of many models of a NEW CORSET, the

W. B. NUFORM

which embodies all the splendid features of the Erect Form and differs but slightly from that excellent garment. The Nuform marks the return to favor of a somewhat higher bust effect and a more slender waist line. It will especially appeal to those women who have found the extremely low bust inadequate for their figures.

W. B. Nuform 403 Average Model This corset has the new high bust effect. Straight front, gives a very slender effect to the waist; medium long hip, front and side supporters. Of white or drab coutil, white batiste or net. Sizes 18 to 30. Price............ **$1**

W. B. Nuform 406 Medium Model Has the new bust and very long hips with unboned apron extension. Reduces waist and hips. Made of strong coutil in white and drab or white batiste. Front and side supporters. Sizes 19 to 30. Price.......... **$1.50**

W. B. Erect Form 929 Stout Model Made with stitched fan front to restrain and flatten abdomen; low bust, deep over hip and abdomen. Of sterling jean in white and drab, black sateen and white batiste. Sizes 19 to 30. Price........... **$1.50** This model also made in $1 and $2.50 qualities.

W. B. Erect Form 952 Slender Model For slim and petite women. The bust is cut low and the hips are not too long. Made in a number of qualities retailing up to $2.50. Style 952 is made of white or drab coutil and white batiste. Sizes 18 to 24. Price........ **$1**

W. B. Erect Form 720 Average Model Is a splendid corset for nine out of ten figures. Has low bust and deep hip. One of the best fitting models of the Erect Form line. Made of an unusually nice quality of coutil in white or drab as well as white batiste. Front and side supporters. Sizes 18 to 30. Price.......

All of these models, as well as numerous other styles in Erect Form and Nuform Corsets, may be found at your retailer's at prices ranging from $1 to $5 the pair. If you cannot obtain them mention dealer's name and send direct to

WEINGARTEN BROTHERS, Dept. E, 377-379 Broadway, New York

The changes in figure and corset changes throughout the early 1900s are too nuanced for most people to detect today, but were considered vital to dressing well, as this 1905 W. B. ad stresses.

From a 1905 Warner's ad that proclaimed, "Fashion says that waists are smaller, decidedly round, the lines rather taping, with the bust higher…This type of form may be easily obtained from the shaping of a Warner's Rust-Proof…Price, one to five dollars per pair."

A 1905 W. B. corset ad, showing some of their most popular styles. The Nuform 403 and Erect Form 720 were considered suitable for "average figures" and were made of white or drab coutil and white batiste. They both sold for $1. The Nuform 406 was better for "medium figures" and was described as having a "deep hip with unboned apron extension, staunch enough to restrain the overfleshiness of hips and abdomen." It sold for $1.50 or $2, depending upon the size.

Royal Worcester corset ad from the October 1905 issue of *The Delineator*.

Whalebone and steel were used in most corsets of this period, but this 1905 La Luette ad boasts the use of "walohn," a man-made "bone" mentioned well into the 1910s.

A 1906 French ad stressing flexibility for active women.

Corsets from the Jackson Corset Company, selling in 1905 for $1 to $1.50.

An unusual corset from 1905, featuring an abdominal belt.

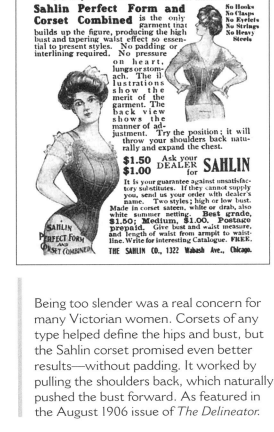

Being too slender was a real concern for many Victorian women. Corsets of any type helped define the hips and bust, but the Sahlin corset promised even better results—without padding. It worked by pulling the shoulders back, which naturally pushed the bust forward. As featured in the August 1906 issue of *The Delineator.*

Corsets for "spirited" women, by C/B in 1906.

Promising to reduce the figure— especially the abdomen—of the stout woman "without the slightest discomfort," the Nemo Self-Reducing Corset sold for $3 in 1906.

"The body needs support" a 1906 Ferris Good Sense Waist ad claimed. But compressing corsets made the body rebel; a Ferris Good Sense Waist, the manufacturer claimed, is flexible, and only gently aids nature.

W. B. corsets advertised widely throughout the late 19th and early 20th centuries, and made a wide variety of corset styles, hoping to please women of all figure types. This ad appeared in the September 1906 issue of *The Ladies Home Journal*.

A Faultless Figure

has the long lines, well accentuated round waist, modified hips and a graceful waist line. All these and from two to four inches longer waist are given by the

G-D *Justrite* CORSET.

In the variety of models offered by this scientifically designed corset, every fault is corrected, every good line and graceful curve brought out.

Ask at the corset department for G-D Justrite. Have several styles fitted to you until you find *your corset*. If a store does not keep the G-D Justrite *don't* buy an inferior corset. Write us and we will see that you are supplied *at once*. The extreme comfort and the attractiveness of your figure in a G-D Justrite make it *pay you to insist upon getting this corset*.

Our "Corset Book" is the latest authority on the correct lines of the figure. We send it *free*.

Gage-Downs Co., 265 Fifth Ave., Chicago

A 1906 ad for G-D Justrite corsets promised a "faultless figure."

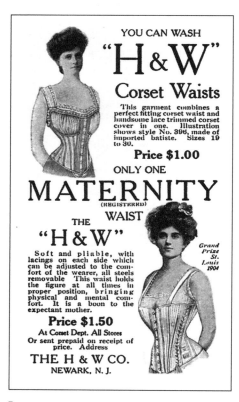

YOU CAN WASH

"H & W" Corset Waists

This garment combines a perfect fitting corset waist and handsome lace trimmed corset cover in one. Illustration shows style No. 396, made of imported batiste. Sizes 19 to 30.

Price $1.00

ONLY ONE

MATERNITY
(REGISTERED)

THE **WAIST**

"H & W"

Soft and pliable, with lacings on each side which can be adjusted to the comfort of the wearer, all steels removable. This waist holds the figure at all times in proper position, bringing physical and mental comfort. It is a boon to the expectant mother.

Grand Prize St. Louis 1904

Price $1.50

At Corset Dept. All Stores Or sent prepaid on receipt of price. Address

THE H & W CO.
NEWARK, N. J.

A 1906 H & W corset ad featuring a maternity corset of "soft and pliable" material, with adjustable lacing along the sides.

A Perfect Figure to Every Lady
WHO WEARS A
Sahlin Perfect Form and Corset Combined

Ladies who have worn this garment are anxious to testify to its merits. The illustrations tell what space does not allow us to print. The Back View shows the manner of adjustment; try the position. It will naturally throw your chest forward, shoulders back and cause you to stand erect—thus broadening the chest, expanding the lungs and strengthening the heart and stomach.

No Hooks
No Clasps
No Eyelets
No Strings
No Heavy Steels

$1.00
$1.50

Ask your dealer for **SAHLIN** It is your guarantee against unsatisfactory substitutes. If he cannot supply you, send us your order with dealer's name. Two styles: high or low bust. Made in corset sateen, white or drab, also white summer netting. **Best grade $1.50; medium $1.00. Postage prepaid.** Give bust and waist measure and length of waist from armpit to waist line. Write for interesting catalogue. Free.

THE SAHLIN COMPANY
1326 Wabash Avenue, Chicago

Designed to "throw your chest forward, shoulders back, and cause you to stand erect," the Sahlin corset sold for between $1 and $1.50 in 1906.

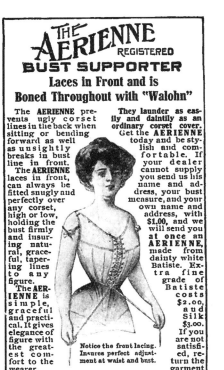

THE AERIENNE REGISTERED
BUST SUPPORTER
Laces in Front and is
Boned Throughout with "Walohn"

The AERIENNE prevents ugly corset lines in the back when sitting or bending forward as well as unsightly breaks in bust line in front. The AERIENNE laces in front, can always be fitted snugly and perfectly over any corset, high or low, holding the bust firmly and insuring natural, graceful, tapering lines to any figure. The AERIENNE is simple, graceful and practical. It gives elegance of figure with the greatest comfort to the wearer.

AERIENNE Bust Supporters can be washed, boiled and ironed without removing the boning.

They launder as easily and daintily as an ordinary corset cover. Get the AERIENNE today and be stylish and comfortable. If your dealer cannot supply you send us his name and address, your bust measure, and your own name and address, with $1.00, and we will send you at once an AERIENNE, made from dainty white Batiste. Extra fine grade of Batiste costs $2.00, and Silk $3.00. If you are not satisfied, return the garment and your money will be cheerfully refunded. Address Dept. 1

Notice the front lacing. Insures perfect adjustment at waist and bust.

LILY OF FRANCE CORSET CO., Inc.,
625 BROADWAY,   **NEW YORK**

Attempting to find favor with those looking for an alternative to rigid, traditional corsets, this 1908 Aerienne ad calls its product a "bust supporter."

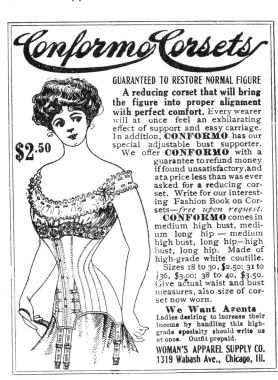

Conformo Corsets

$2.50

GUARANTEED TO RESTORE NORMAL FIGURE

A reducing corset that will bring the figure into proper alignment with perfect comfort. Every wearer will at once feel an exhilarating effect of support and easy carriage. In addition, **CONFORMO** has our special adjustable bust supporter. We offer **CONFORMO** with a guarantee to refund money if found unsatisfactory, and at a price less than was ever asked for a reducing corset. Write for our interesting Fashion Book on Corsets—*free upon request.* **CONFORMO** comes in medium high bust, medium long hip — medium high bust, long hip—high bust, long hip. Made of high-grade white coutille. Sizes 18 to 30, $2.50; 31 to 36, $3.00; 38 to 40, $3.50. Give actual waist and bust measures, also size of corset now worn.

We Want Agents

Ladies desiring to increase their income by handling this high-grade **specialty** should write us at once. Outfit prepaid.

WOMAN'S APPAREL SUPPLY CO.
1319 Wabash Ave., Chicago, Ill.

W.B. Reduso CORSETS

The supreme in corsets—

REDUSO, ERECT FORM and NUFORM, imparting shapeliness to the largest as well as the slenderest of women.

THE REDUSO FOR LARGE WOMEN

Fleshiness need not be unbecoming

The **REDUSO** will improve the figure of over-developed women. It accomplishes remarkable results with the greatest ease, effecting a positive reduction of from **one to five inches**, entirely by its scientific construction and entirely without the aid of cumbersome straps or harness-like devices.

REDUSO, Style 770 (as pictured) for tall, large women. Made of very serviceable white coutil or batiste with three pairs hose supporters. Sizes 19 to 36. **PRICE $3.00.**

REDUSO, Style 772—for short, large women. Made of durable white coutil and batiste, same construction and hose supporters as style 770. Sizes 19 to 36. **PRICE $3.00.**

REDUSO, Style 774—a most desirable corset for tall, large women. Made about one inch longer below the waist-line than style 770, but of a material specially woven to withstand extreme wear and strain. Three pairs hose supporters. Sizes 19 to 36. **PRICE $5.00.**

REDUSO, Style 775—another model for tall, large women. This garment is perfection in all essentials of this type of corset. Fabric is the finest self-striped imported coutil, richly trimmed and especially boned to insure extra flexibility and undoubted strength. Sizes 19 to 36. **PRICE $10.00.**

NUFORM No 463 · $1 00

Reduso No 770 · $3 00

W. B. NUFORM—THE HIP-SUBDUING CORSET

That precise hip fit to your costumes and gowns, the "long figure" effect, is entirely dependent on the correctness of the corset you wear. Wherever the full benefit of a corset is desired, the NUFORM or the ERECT FORM is sure to prove the pride of the wardrobe. These corsets are made in a great variety of shapes, insuring an absolute fit for every type of figure.

EXTRA—The W. B. "BEAUTY BOOK"—the most fascinating booklet compiled—containing many pages of health-giving advice—interesting statistics about the perfect form—the use and making of beautifiers at home—the art of lacing and corset fitting, and valuable information about improving the face and figure. Profusely illustrated and artistically printed. Mailed **FREE** upon request.

NUFORM, Style 463—the average tall woman will find this corset especially suitable. Made of white coutil and batiste. Hose supporters front and sides. Sizes 18 to 30. **PRICE $1.00.**

Also made in $1.50, $2.00 and $3.00 qualities.

Ask any dealer anywhere to show you any of the models described here and the many other equally attractive styles.

WEINGARTEN BROS., Makers, 377-379 Broadway, New York.

At the turn of the century, and for many years before and after that time, to be either overweight or too slender was considered equally unfortunate. W. B. ran this 1908 ad targeting larger women, saying their Reduso corset made women up to 5 inches thinner. Since corsets tended to make hips large, they also stress their corset is "hip-subduing."

Although corsets were worn by fashionably-sized women, too, this 1908 corset ad targets overweight women.

Are You Getting Stout?

You can have as good a figure as any woman if you wear one of my **Ewing Reducing Garments** and you need not diet, take drugs or tiresome exercises. I make the Ewing Hip and Abdominal Reducing Band, and the Ewing Bust Reducing Garment. They are beautifully made of light materials, lined with thin rubber, ventilated, cool and comfortable to wear. No buckles, straps or steels. They will reduce you 4 to 14 inches the first time worn and without the slightest harm or inconvenience. I make them to your measure to reduce just the parts you wish. Every garment guaranteed. No corset can reduce you permanently, and no other Reducing Garments are hygienic and comfortable — I know because I have tried them all. The Ewing Reducing Garments do not bind or distribute the flesh to other parts—they **draw the fat completely away.** The Ewing Hip and Abdominal Reducer weighs **only 5 oz.** Sold and recommended by the leading dry goods stores in Chicago. Endorsed by eminent Physicians and hundreds of men and women wearers. Wear the band a few weeks before having your fall gowns made.

Send 2-cent stamp for my illustrated booklet and measurement blanks. Don't go a week longer without knowing what I can do for you. Society women, leading women of the stage, and men and women in all walks of life are my satisfied and grateful patrons. **ELIZABETH EWING, Dept. F-W, 1000 Sheffield Ave., Chicago**

Although technically not a corset, this "reducing band" was similar. Meant to control rounded stomachs, it was essentially a rubber girdle, advertised in 1908.

A Graceful Figure

is woman's most lasting charm. Cultivate and preserve it by wearing the

G-D Justrite CORSETS

NO. 2020

Whatever your figure, the **G-D Justrite** naturally produces the now desired round, slender waist and hip effect. It slopes gently and gracefully *in* at the waist line, leaving plenty of room for deep breathing. It has the perfect hip. Each model shapes the form to the lines of *its* ideal.

For Every Form there's a *Justrite* Fit

Ask your Dealer to show you the G-D Justrite Model that is just right for YOU. Write us for FREE CORSET BOOK a complete guide to corset selection

GAGE-DOWNS COMPANY
268 Fifth Avenue - Chicago, Ill.

Judging by advertisements of the era, including this 1908 G-D Justrite ad, by the early 1900s women were more interested in being able to breathe while wearing a corset.

STYLISH WOMEN WEAR

BON TON CORSETS

EVERY corset virtue is fully expressed in the exquisite new Spring models.

Among other exclusive features, those distinctively new are the high bust, long flat front, long shapely back, and the very new, long flat hip effect, Fashion's latest requirements.

$3 TO $10 SOLD EVERYWHERE

ROYAL WORCESTER CORSET CO.

WORCESTER   NEW YORK
CHICAGO   SAN FRANCISCO

MAKERS OF

ROYAL WORCESTER AND BON TON CORSETS

"Bon Ton" (meaning "the fashionable elite") was a term adopted by many fashion makers, including those of the Bon Ton corset. This ad is from the May 1908 issue of *The Delineator*.

Warner's Rust-Proof Corsets

*D*O you know that the boning, clasps, side steels and backbone of *Warner's* Corsets are guaranteed not to rust, break or punch through the fabric and that the eyelets cannot rust or pull out? The question is most satisfactorily answered by wearing.

The way a corset is put on has much to do with the shaping and everything with the comfort. Properly selected and properly fitted a Warner's Corset is without a parallel.

We have a little folder which has been prepared by the designers of these noted corsets, which not only tells you how to adjust and wear these corsets, but how to care for corsets. Send for this helpful folder. There are more than fifty styles in Warner's Corsets, and there are enough of these styles carried by retailers everywhere to guarantee a perfect fit for every size form, from the slimmest to the stoutest.

Security Rubber Button Hose Supporters attached to every pair.

$1.00 to $5.00 Per Pair

The Warner Bros. Co., New York, Chicago, Oakland

EVERY PAIR GUARANTEED

Even though corsets were seen only by the women who wore them, their maids, and perhaps their husbands, having them in disrepair was not acceptable—even if the eyelets were slightly rusted from wear or cleaning. As seen in this 1908 *Delineator* ad.

W.B. CORSETS

W. B. REDUSO
The perfect corset for large women

It places over-developed women on the same basis as their slender sisters. By its scientific construction it tapers off the bust, and absolutely reduces the abdomen and hips from 1 to 5 inches, without the aid of torturing straps or harness-like devices.

NEW W. B. REDUSO No. 770.—For Large Tall Women. Made of white coutil. Hose supporters front and sides. Sizes 20 to 36. PRICE $3.00.

NEW W. B. REDUSO No. 771. — Is the same as No. 770 but made of light weight white batiste. Hose supporters front and sides. Sizes 20 to 36. PRICE $3.00.

NEW W. B. REDUSO No. 772 for Large Short Women is the same as No. 770 except that the bust is somewhat lower all around. Made of white coutil. Hose supporters front and sides. Sizes 20 to 36. PRICE $3.00.

NEW W. B. REDUSO No. 773. Is the same as No. 772, but made of light weight white batiste. Hose supporters front and sides. Sizes 20 to 36. PRICE $3.00.

THE NEW W. B. "HIP-SUBDUING" MODELS

will produce the correct figure for prevailing modes. The scientific construction of W. B. Corsets has never been as thoroughly demonstrated as in the garments illustrated herewith.

These corsets in a very extensive range of models are constructed to produce for figures varying from extreme stoutness to unusual slenderness the graceful hip lines necessary as a foundation for the prevailing clinging gowns and the general long line appearance which is characteristic of the very modish woman.

From $1.00 to $3.00 the pair.
WEINGARTEN BROS., Mfrs.,
377-379 B'way, New York

Nuform 446

For well-developed figures, is a reverse gore model. The gore lines run backwards, a construction which restrains undue development below the back. Medium high bust, long hips and extra long back. Made of an excellent quality of white coutil and white batiste. Hose supporters front and sides. Sizes 19 to 30. PRICE $2.00. *Also made in $3.00 quality.*

Ask any dealer anywhere to show you the corsets illustrated on this page, or any of our numerous styles, which are made in such a variety as to guarantee a perfect fit for every type of figure.

Nuform 406

Is a splendid corset for medium figures. Medium high bust and deep hip, ending in an unboned apron extension. Made of white and drab coutil and white batiste. Hose supporters front and sides. Sizes 18 to 30. PRICE $1.50.

Also made in $2.00 and $3.00 qualities.

ERECT FORM 753.—A corset for average figures. Has medium bust and long hip. Made of white and drab coutil and white batiste. Hose supporters on front and sides. Sizes 18 to 30. PRICE $1.00.

W. B. corset ads, like this one from the May 1908 issue of *The Delineator,* often targeted slender or "stout" women.

How to Gain a Graceful Figure

Slenderness Depends largely on a Correct Fit of Clothes and Corset

By MILLICENT MARVIN

IT SEEMS to be the object of all women, just now, to become slender, for women of pronounced embonpoint have not been taken into consideration by the designers of the new corsets. They will have to struggle along as best they can and modify their figures gradually.

It is the slim woman and the one that is just plump enough to look well who are the chief concern as well as the great joy of the *corsetiere* and modiste. They have no bulging hips to reduce and none of the other trials of the very stout person. It is commonly believed that the only way to reduce the apparent size of the hips is by lacing them up in very tight corsets. This really only makes them look larger. There are ways of arranging and adjusting other lines of the figure so that one looks almost sylph-like. It is a study, however, requiring much thought and consideration. I shall be very glad to send general suggestions and rules concerning these lines to any woman who will send me her height and weight, enclosing a self-addressed, stamped envelope for a reply. I also will be pleased to send a very effective hip-reducing exercise that will work wonders in helping one to get rid of bulging hips.

An exercise for a supple waist

The Importance of Sitting Properly

It is through sitting properly—directions for which may be had for the asking,—exercising and eating, or rather avoiding certain kinds of food, that one may reduce weight. Proper sitting will also do much towards reducing a prominent abdomen, as the wrong position pushes it forward and disproportionately develops it.

Many women have the habit of sitting or leaning in a one-sided fashion, which sooner or later shows its results in the shoulders and hips. This is especially so with those whose duties compel them to sit several hours daily in front of a desk.

There is also a tendency among women to a drooping position when standing. The back should be flat, that is, the shoulder-blades should not protrude, and with the exercise of proper care there is no reason why they should.

Under the straight front régime, the hips were made to look smaller because the waist was larger; but fashion has decreed that the small waist is the thing, and the hour of the long, extremely long-waisted woman is at hand.

There is absolutely no doubt that either a fat woman or an extremely thin one may be given a charming outline by wearing the correct style of corset. It is always an excellent plan for the woman with a large figure to be well fitted to this boned article of dress, and always to have an eye to its balancing properties.

Never choose a corset that produces a good waistline at the expense of the hips, or a good hip curve to the detriment of the waist.

If you are in doubt as to what style of corset you should wear to improve your figure, and will enclose a self-addressed stamped envelope to this department, I shall be glad to help you.

Waist-Reducing Belts of Rubber

A corset coming well down over the hips will serve to keep down too pronounced plumpness, and it gives a continuity of line that is most desirable in the case of large hips.

New routes to slenderness are opened periodically, and women travel them with all the enthusiasm of which they are capable, hoping above all to gain a slender waist and a pretty figure. The latest waist-reducing fad —the rubber belt —has met with great success. It is simplicity itself in arrangement and adjustment, and its effect is almost instantaneous.

For the most part these waist-reducing belts are of home manufacture. These belts are quite simple and easy to make.

The proper lacing of the corset

They are made of the finest and purest rubber that can be bought. Rubber that the dentists use is excellent on account of its fineness and elasticity, while it will withstand considerable strain. Such rubber is expensive, but it comes wide, and as only a narrow strip is required the actual cost of one of these belts is small.

The belt must be made to fit the individual and its width depends entirely upon the build of the wearer. There are no bones in it and no stiffening is required. Each belt rounds down slightly at the front to suit the figure.

No sane woman is going to risk her health for the sake of reducing her waistline, but she need have no fear of a properly worn rubber belt. The directions for making these belts, as well as a very helpful waist-reducing exercise, may be had by writing to this department.

The main reason for superfluous flesh about the waist is that the muscles there are not used as they should be and therefore become flabby. For this a devitalizing exercise is beneficial.

The new combination garment

Narrow chests, bent shoulders and undeveloped busts are other beauty ills that confront the woman with an ungainly figure. They all tell their own story. The lungs have not been used to their full working capacity, and the unexercised muscles and joints of the upper portion of the body have remained undeveloped.

Breathe Deeply to Develop Your Chest

Chest development is the most beneficial when it comes through regular breathing exercises and a few simple arm and shoulder exercises kept up daily. These exercises may be secured by writing this department. There is no woman with a flat chest, or an undeveloped bust who cannot correct this ill if she chooses.

A pretty pair of shoulders curving out from a graceful neck and sloping down to shapely arms, will always call forth admiration and they, too, can easily be acquired by the right sort of exercise. Their poise, too, must be perfect, and their lines graceful. By writing to this department information will be given how to develop the arms, shoulders and neck into shapely outlines; and recipes for an unguent and a lotion to whiten the skin will be sent.

Sometimes a face as fair as a lily is set above shoulders and arms as rough as a grater and almost as red as the proverbial boiled lobster.

The roughness consists of a pimply surface, the pimples being minute and dry. Such shoulders should be washed every night with warm water and a fine soap or almond meal, a recipe for which may be had by writing for it to this department. After thoroughly drying the shoulders and arms, a good skin food should be applied. I will be glad to send a recipe for an excellent skin food.

Undergarments Should Fit Smoothly

Next in importance to exercise and correct corseting in improving an ungainly figure comes the lingerie worn. A perfect combination has been evolved, the pattern for which may be had for a few cents, which adds practically nothing to either the hip or waist measurement. The combination most in favor is the one which provides corset cover and drawers. The garment is fashioned in several pieces set together with seam binding.

The difference achieved by wearing a combination garment instead of the ordinary arrangement of the separate pieces can readily be appreciated; so many women with large hips stubbornly cling to the old-fashioned garments which cannot fail to make them look bunchy and ungainly.

They have at least three thicknesses at their waistline, while puckers and gathers make ridges where everything should be smooth and trim. A chemise increases the hip circumference at least an inch, while a corset cover ending just above or just below the curve of the hips will add even more. If one can gain two or three inches, or possibly more, by the careful adjustment of the undergarments is it not worth while?

Fortunately for the woman with large hips, it is fashionable to have wide-shouldered gowns. This provides a way to decrease the appearance of the hips considerably.

A correct sitting position

Fashions of the early 1900s favored the young and slim. This 1908 editorial from *The Delineator* discusses how best to wear fashions if the figure is more rounded.

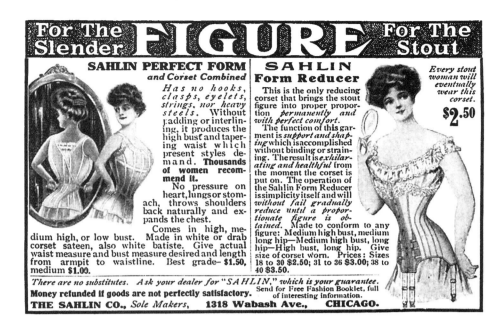

For The Slender FIGURE **For The Stout**

SAHLIN PERFECT FORM
and Corset Combined

Has no hooks, clasps, eyelets, strings, nor heavy steels. Without padding or interlining, it produces the high bust and tapering waist which present styles demand. **Thousands of women recommend it.**

No pressure on heart, lungs or stomach, throws shoulders back naturally and expands the chest.

Comes in high, medium high, or low bust. Made in white or drab corset sateen, also white batiste. Give actual waist measure and bust measure desired and length from armpit to waistline. Best grade– **$1.50,** medium **$1.00.**

There are no substitutes. Ask your dealer for "SAHLIN," which is your guarantee.
Money refunded if goods are not perfectly satisfactory.
THE SAHLIN CO., *Sole Makers,* **1318 Wabash Ave., CHICAGO.**

SAHLIN Form Reducer

This is the only reducing corset that brings the stout figure into proper proportion *permanently and with perfect comfort.*

The function of this garment is *support and shaping* which is accomplished without binding or straining. The result is *exhilarating and healthful* from the moment the corset is put on. The operation of the Sahlin Form Reducer is simplicity itself and will *without fail gradually reduce until a proportionate figure is obtained.* Made to conform to any figure: Medium high bust, medium long hip—Medium high bust, long hip—High bust, long hip. Give size of corset worn. Prices: Sizes 18 to 30 $2.50; 31 to 36 $3.00; 38 to 40 $3.50.

Send for Free Fashion Booklet, full of interesting information.

Every stout woman will eventually wear this corset.
$2.50

This 1908 Sahlin ad promises to either plump or slenderize the figure.

Modern women complain bras create ugly bulges on their back. Women in 1908 complained corsets did the same thing. Enter the Aerienne Bust Supporter, which, among other things, claimed to eliminate this bulge.

Nemo **CORSET SPECIALTIES**

FOR STOUT WOMEN — FOR SLENDER FIGURES

Self-Reducing 312 Long — Self-Reducing 318 Short — Military Belt 301 — Festoon 350 — Swan Shape 355

Nemo corsets for "stout" and "slender" women.

Nemo corsets from a Lipman, Wolfe & Co. catalog, featuring corsets for almost every problem figure.

C/B corsets, selling for between $1 and $5 in the Lipman, Wolfe & Co. catalog. The same catalog also featured mohair and silk corset laces, as well as perspiration shields to protect corsets and dresses.

Ferris Good Sense Waists

T839. Plain Cordea Waist, short; white or drab; sizes 22 to 26 for ages 2 to 5 years; for ages 5 to 8, sizes 22 to 26; price.....25c

T843. Misses' Ferris Waist, 9 to 12 years; jean; button front, laced back; white or drab; sizes 19 to 26; price 75c

T847. Misses' Waist, 12 to 17 years; plaited bust; drab and white; sizes 21 to 26; price, each $1.00

T851. Young Ladies' Ferris Waist, 14 to 17 years; button front; white only; sizes 21 to 26; price $1.00

T805. Fine Cambric Shirred Waist; embroidery or lace and ribbon; 3 to 14 years..50c Similar, plain......25c

T841. Ladies' Athletic Waist, fine batiste; sizes 19 to 26....:.$1.00 In ordering give exact size of corset wanted.

T845. Ladies' Waist, straight front, fine batiste; white only; button front; sizes 20 to 26; price......$1.00

T849. Ladies' Dip Hip Waist; button front; white only; sizes 21 to 28; price $1.00

T853. Ladies' Waist; soft full bust; white batiste; button front; sizes 22 to 26; price, each $1.00

T857. Ladies' Waist; button front; drab only; sizes 22 to 30; price ....$1.00 Sizes 31 to 36....$1.25

Ferris Good Sense Waists, as featured in the Lipman, Wolfe & Co. catalog. The children's corsets were corded and cost just 25¢ and up. The athletic waist was $1. Although reform fashions never caught on for most American women, Ferris corsets were often advertised. They were probably worn by women involved in sporting activities or by young children.

W. B. corsets, as featured in the Lipman, Wolfe & Co. catalog of the early 1900s.

A naughty photo of the early 1900s, showing a lounging woman with a shockingly small waist.

A suggestive French drawing from the early 1900s, showing two men tightening a woman's corset.

A French corset from the turn of the century.

Women could tighten their own corsets by crossing the strings in the back and pulling them around the front of the waist.

The C/B Spirite corset was popular at the turn of the century.

A long corset for the new Regency-style fashions of the early 1900s.

A maternity corset featured in a *Bon Marché* catalog from the early 1900s.

An early 1900s Coronet corset ad, showing how "superior" a new style corset was to the figure.

A maternity corset with elastic at the hips and laces in back and on the sides.

A racy photograph postcard from the early 1900s, showing a woman removing a ribbon corset. These short corsets were made of strips of cloth or ribbon and were designed primarily for sportswear.

A woman cinching in her waist with a S-curve corset. Notice how the corset has an open area at center front; this is designed to help create the "pigeon bosom" so popular at this time.

Madame Bellanger corsets, as seen in a 1910 issue of *La Mode Illustrée*.

Warner Brothers began in 1874 and was run by two women's disease "specialists." Warner's continued making corsets and other lingerie through the late 1960s, when the business diversified and changed its name. This corset was featured in the September 1910 issue of *Ladies' Home Journal*.

A typical long line corset of the 1910s.

LE
CORSET
PERSÉPHONE

N° 910

Ce merveilleux corset
qui vous engaine d'une façon
si parfaite, vous assure, Madame,
même avec une robe très simple:

*LA SUPRÊME ÉLÉGANCE
& LA PLUS JEUNE ALLURE*

Il a, en outre, ce très réel avantage
de vous procurer, par sa construction ingénieuse

*UNE AISANCE TOUT A
FAIT EXCEPTIONNELLE*

EN TRÈS JOLI TISSU PÈKINÈ. PRIX. 29 FRANCS.
CHEZ

BATBY 187. Rue St Honoré PARIS
Mᵐᵉ BOISSIÈRE. 21. Rue de la République. ROUEN
Mᵐᵉ DAVID 75. Rue de Paris. LE HAVRE
Mᵐᵉ MILLETRE. 24 Rue du Calvaire. NANTES.

The new, long corset, as it appeared in an ad in the June 12, 1910 issue of *La Mode Illustrée*.

A corset for a young teen, from 1911.

A 1912 ad for a French corset.

A 1912 Ferris corset without boning. It was stiffened with less restrictive cording.

W. B. Reduso CORSETS

W. B. NUFORM CORSETS

combine style perfection and fit with comfort, at popular prices. They fit the figure with the exactness of custom tailoring, and afford most effective foundations for fashionable gowns. A large variety of individual designs is provided in all sizes and lengths, so that every woman can find a model specially adapted to her requirements, giving the figure superb, graceful lines.

W. B. NUFORM CORSETS are firmly boned, retain permanently their perfect lines and are guaranteed to give satisfaction. NUFORM boning will not rust.

Made of specially woven fabrics, both in light and heavy weight, attractively finished with lace, embroidery, ribbon, and hose supporters.

W. B. REDUSO CORSETS

do not squeeze, do not force, do not press the figure. Without the aid of any strap or attachment,—simply by the scientific arrangement and placing of the gores, the W. B. REDUSO actually accomplishes the remarkable reduction of **one to five inches** in the measurement of hips and abdomen, without pressure or discomfort.

Extra durable fabrics, firm boning and splendid tailoring enable W. B. REDUSO CORSETS to retain their shape indefinitely. They are made in a variety of models to insure a perfect fit for tall, medium and short, developed figures.

The W. B. REDUSO ingeniously supports the fullness of the figure and bust, producing most graceful outlines.

NUFORM, Style 478. The extremely popular W. B. $1.00 long corset. Medium bust, very long hips and back. Made of wear-defying coutil, prettily trimmed. Hose supporters attached.
Sizes 18-30.
Price, $1.00

NUFORM, Style 485. —(As pictured). For average figures. Medium bust height, long over hips, back and abdomen. Material is durable coutil. 2 pairs hose supporters attached.
Sizes 18-30.
Price, $1.50

NUFORM, Style 109. A splendid model for tall average figures. High in bust, long over hips, back and abdomen. The material is excellent coutil. 3 pairs hose supporters attached.
Sizes 18-30.
Price, $2.00

NUFORM, Style 114. A superb model for average or well developed figures. High bust —not extreme —long over hips, back and abdomen. Imported coutil, embroidery trimming. 3 pairs hose supporters attached.
Sizes 18-30.
Price, $3.00

NUFORM, Style 118. A low bust model, very long over hips and back, especially built for the comfort of well developed and stout figures. Imported coutil. Lace trimming. 3 pairs hose supporters attached. **Price, $3.00**

The above models, as well as many other Nuform and Erect Form styles, are shown by all dealers.

REDUSO, Style 782. —(As pictured). A remarkable model for tall, large figures. The bust height is medium. The hips, back and abdomen are very long. The slashes at bottom of corset insure perfect comfort. 3 pairs hose supporters.
Sizes 19-36.
Price, $5.00

REDUSO, Style 781. The ideal corset for short, stout figures. Exceptionally low under the arms, long over hips, back and abdomen. Made of service-giving coutil. 3 pairs hose supporters.
Sizes 19-36.
Price, $3.00

REDUSO, Style 770. For average well developed figures. Medium high bust, long over hips and abdomen. Made of durable white batiste or coutil. 3 pairs hose supporters.
Sizes 19-36.
Price, $3.00

REDUSO, Style 776. For tall, well developed figures. The bust is high, the hips, back and abdomen very long. Made of very excellent coutil or batiste. 3 pairs hose supporters.
Sizes 19-36.
Price, $3.00

REDUSO, Style 779. Medium low bust, quite long over hips and back. The material is a staunchly woven striped REDUSO Cloth. 3 pairs hose supporters.
Sizes 19-36.
Price, $4.00

Above Reduso models are sold by dealers everywhere.

NUFORM № 485 $1.50   Reduso № 782 $5.00

W. B. FORMU CORSETS give a full bust effect to figures of slight bust development. Style 107—$2.00. Style 112—$2.50. Style 113—$3.00

WEINGARTEN BROS., Makers, 34th Street and Broadway, NEW YORK

The fashion for less rigid corsets died when long, lean fashions took hold. Now it was more common for corset manufacturers to brag their corsets were "firmly boned" and wouldn't become misshapen, as with this ad from a 1910 issue of *Ladies' Home Journal.*

Newest corset design, 1917.

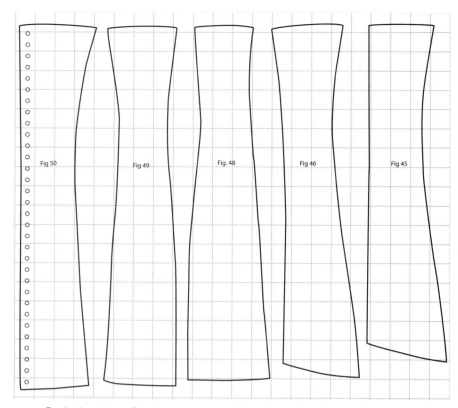

Fig 50   Fig 49   Fig. 48   Fig 46   Fig 45

Scaled pattern for the same corset, redrawn for the modern sewer.
1 square = 1"

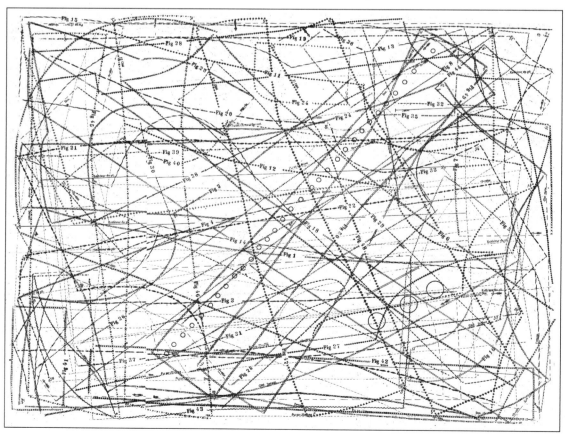

Pattern as presented in the June 3, 1917 issue of *La Mode Illustree*.

Corded—not boned—corsets by Ferris, designed just for girls of 1912.

A 1913 image showing how necessary it was to have long corsets with the new lean fashions.

An American Lady corset for "medium figures, low bust, extra long hip, extra long back, batiste…$2" in 1912.

The Corset
that supports &
reduces

LEADING doctors and specialists have testified to the health-value of this wonderful yet simple corset, and their opinions are further endorsed by the fact that hundreds of the most notable of fashion's devotees wear them regularly. Prices range from 6/11 to 45/-.

Send for the Free Book describing and illustrating the Jenyn's Patent Reducing and Supporting Corset to-day.

**Corsets, Box 185, G.P.O.,
MANCHESTER**

The JENYNS' PATENT
REDUCING & SUPPORTING CORSET
Patent Nos. 16014/1910 & 4597/1912

With its many laces and clasps, this 1913 corset was designed to slim the stomach and hips for the long, lean dresses of the period.

"TREO" TRIUMPHS

THE "TREO" GIRDLE

MADE entirely of porous woven surgical elastic web, which "gives" freely to every movement of the body, yet firmly holds the figure. Lends grace with absolute comfort. Our patented method of construction and character of materials used make it equally desirable for street, dancing, evening or sport wear; white or flesh tint.' Retail, Misses' lengths, $3.00 to $7.50; Adults lengths, $4.00 to $10.00.

CAUTION. The TREO GIRDLE has the feature strip of elastic above the elastic waist-line band, and, therefore, supports the body above and below the waist-line. Other similar all-elastic garments are simply hip-confiners, and Not Elastic Corsets. *If your dealer cannot supply you, write for FREE Booklet.*

TREO "Paraknit" Brassiere

is made of "Paraknit," a new kind of light weight, open work, elastic material, invented by us which is very, very flexible, extremely stylish, and healthful.

Reinforced elastic diaphragm strip at lower edge supports and reduces diaphragm without pressure, and is a very great advantage. *Retail $2 and $2.50 at dealers, or write for illustrated booklet.*

TREO COMPANY, Inc.
160-B Fifth Avenue - - - - - New York
In Canada, Address, EISMAN & CO., Toronto

"TREO" GIRDLE
The All-Elastic Corset
With the Feature Strip

"TREO" Paraknit
Elastic Brassiere
Reinforced Diaphragm Strip

Now that the tango and similar dances were common, corsets had to allow better freedom of movement. And as corsets became more like girdles, brassieres were often sold alongside them, as in this 1919 ad.

——it's the same with hats,

some make you look younger—just so with Corsets.

YOU do look younger when you are correctly corseted. Be wise and wear a G-D Justrite Corset which has been designed over a living model with ideal figure lines.

Select the style of G-D Justrite for your figure type and in continuing to wear it, your figure is molded into the same outline. You will surely see this change. *IT'S THE G-D JUSTRITE DESIGNING DOES IT.*

Priced from $25 down, according to material.

There is a Model designed for your type of figure. Good stores and Corset Shops sell G-D Justrite Corsets. Free Booklet "Corset Secrets."

GAGE-DOWNS COMPANY, Dept. C

Makers of G-D Justrite Corsets. 2706 Wabash Ave., Chicago

G-D *Justrite* Corsets

The 1910s were the beginning of fashion's love of all things youthful, and this 1919 ad promised to make women look younger if only they'd wear a G-D Justrite corset.

Prospective Mothers

H&W
Maternity
No. 2215
$3.50

very prospective mother may have a stylish appearance, safety for the little one and comfort for herself during the maternity period. For twenty-five years the H. & W. Maternity Corset Waist has been by far the most favored product in this highly popular line.

It gives support where most needed, is soft and pliable, with lacings on either side adjustable to the comfort of the wearer, and thus after confinement, as well as before, holds the figure stylishly and naturally.

Particularly, also, is it invaluable after surgical operations and in every convalescence, correcting weaknesses and properly preserving the figure at all times with perfect safety and comfort.

Made in a variety of styles and prices. We especially recommend Number 2215, here illustrated. Price $3.50 at all dealers. If your dealer hasn't it, write and we will see that you are supplied.

Write for booklet

The H. & W. Co., Newark, N. J.

LET your mirror reflect you at your best. You cannot do yourself justice unless you wear a perfect fitting corset.

THOMSON'S
"Glove-Fitting"
CORSETS

AMONG the latest models is one which will give *your* figure those slender youthful lines.

"The Standard Corset of the World" for 64 years.

GEO. C. BATCHELLER & CO.
130 Fifth Ave., New York
Chicago   San Francisco

A maternity corset from 1919, designed for "a stylish appearance, safety for the little one and comfort" for the mother.

MODART CORSETS
Front Laced

MODART CORSETS
ALWAYS FRONT LACED

The preference of the best stores nearly everywhere to *feature* the Modart is but the reflection of the satisfaction this truly remarkable corset has given to their most valued patrons.

MODART CORSET COMPANY, SAGINAW, MICHIGAN

There is No Other Corset Like the Modart

A Trial Fitting is *proof*—and your first step toward a better figure.

Supreme lasting comfort from the moment you leave the fitting room.

Economy is assured. Modart wearing qualities will amaze you. Your Modart will keep its shape until entirely worn out.

And remember, a corset that won't keep its own lines cannot maintain yours.

Laundering won't hurt it in the least.

Consider style, comfort, wear—most of all consider your figure.

Do you want any but the best corset?

Modart ads always stressed a proper fitting, and their saleswomen were trained to take "scientific measurements." This ad appeared in the September 1919 issue of *Ladies' Home Journal.*

A Thomson's Glove-Fitting Corsets ad from 1919—64 years in the corset business.

A 1910s era maternity corset—not much more modern than those during the Victorian period.

A Spirella corset from the 1910s.

An "athletic" corset from the 1910s.

A 1910s era racy photograph showing a long corset with garters attached.

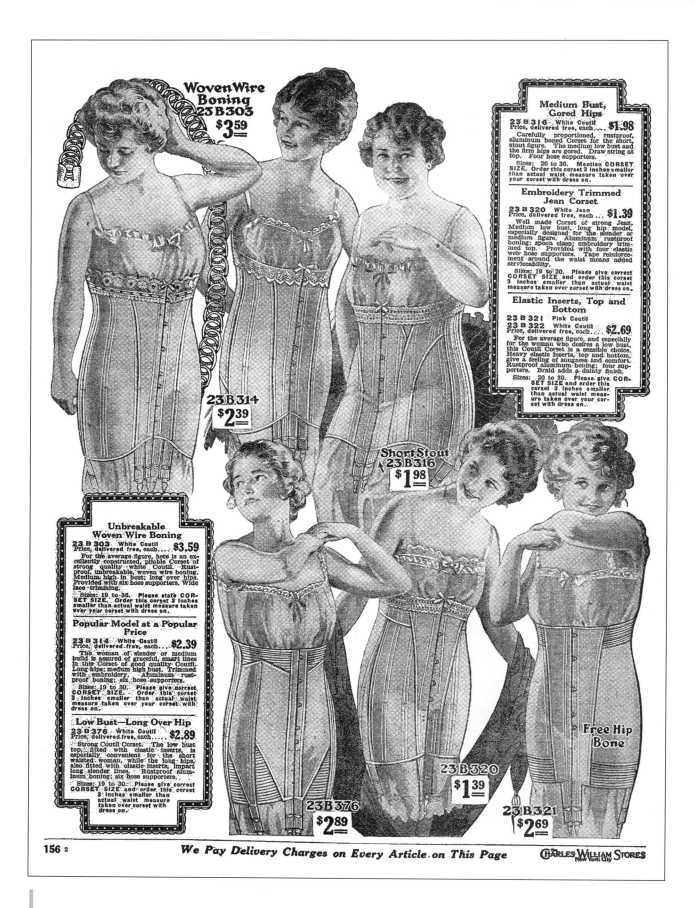

Woven Wire Boning
23B303 $3⁵⁹

23B314 $2³⁹

Short Stout 23B316 $1⁹⁸

23B376 $2⁸⁹

23B320 $1³⁹

Free Hip Bone

23B321 $2⁶⁹

We Pay Delivery Charges on Every Article on This Page

Charles William Stores New York City

"Woven wire boning" was more flexible than flat steel bones or feather or
whalebone. As seen in a *Charles William Stores* catalog from the 1910s.

Ventilated Back 23B312
$2 59

Reducer 23B346
$3 98

Reduces Over-Developed Abdomen

23 B 346 White Coutil
Price, delivered free, each.....................$3.98

Cleverly designed right-fitting Corset for the stout woman who wishes to reduce with ease and comfort. Made in the convenient and practical front lacing style of strong Coutil, featuring a reinforced front portion and two elastic bands which control the abdomen and facilitate reducing. Embroidery finished top; six strong elastic web hose supporters.

Sizes: 20 to 36. Please give CORSET SIZE. Order this corset 1 inch smaller than actual waist measure taken over your corset with dress on.

Approved Form Fitting Corset

23 B 358 Flesh Color, Brocaded Sateen
Price, delivered free, each.....................$3.98

A comfortable Corset in a fine quality Brocaded Sateen that wears satisfactorily. Inserts of elastic webbing at top and around hips give that snugness most women seek. Made in new front lacing style with a low bust line, and medium long back and hips. Silk braid trimming. Rustproof duplex aluminum boning. Six elastic web hose supporters.

Sizes: 19 to 30. Please give CORSET SIZE and order this corset 1 inch smaller than actual waist measure taken over your corset with dress on.

Brocaded Sateen Front Lacing Style

23 B 309 White Brocaded Sateen
23 B 310 Flesh Color, Brocaded
Price, delivered free, each.....................$3.98

The medium, well developed figure finds the utmost comfort in this skilfully designed Corset of good quality Brocaded Sateen with pliant, rustproof aluminum boning throughout. Front lacing style. Six elastic web hose supporters. Tricot and rubber inserts in back for added comfort. Lace and ribbon trimming.

Sizes: 19 to 30. Please give CORSET SIZE. Order this corset 1 inch smaller than actual waist measure taken over your corset with dress on.

23B382
$2 49

Ventilated Back Brocade 23B309
$3 98

An Ideal Corset for Medium Figures

23 B 312 White Coutil
Price, delivered free, each **$2.59**

A very substantial model in a front lacing Corset is this good quality White Coutil, strongly stayed with aluminum rustproof boning. Tape reinforcement around the waist. Medium high bust, long hips and high back. For healthful comfort the strip of tricot mesh has been inserted up the back. A drawstring adjusts the medium low bust. Four elastic hose supporters. Lace trimmed top.

Sizes: 19 to 30. Please state CORSET SIZE. Order this corset 1 inch smaller than actual waist measure taken over your corset with dress on.

Smart Lines Good Fitting

23 B 382 White Coutil
Price, delivered free, each **$2.49**

The slender or medium figure will find unusual grace and smartness in this excellent quality Coutil Corset. Made in a popular and practical front lacing style with inserts of elastic at top to provide added flexibility. Firm, rustproof aluminum boning throughout. Four elastic hose supporters. Hooks below front stays prevent accidental opening.

Sizes: 19 to 30. Please state CORSET SIZE. Order this corset 1 inch smaller than actual waist measure taken over your corset with dress on.

Brocade 23B358
$3 98

CHARLES WILLIAM STORES
New York City

We Pay Delivery Charges on Every Article on This Page

155

Corsets for a medium figure, as seen in a *Charles William Stores* catalog.

A flexible, slightly boned corset made in soft Goodwinette fabric, giving the natural lines to the body. It is the acme of comfort and service.

ATHLETIC. A light, low top corset, adapted from the T model, which may be used for athletics or regular wear.

A lightly boned corset designed for the youthful or slight figure and for sensitive persons who need very little corseting.

A short, very lightly boned corset for misses and those with slight figures.

Just as doctors once recommended certain brands of cigarettes, doctors also once recommended certain makes of corsets as seen on these 2 pages. In 1922, Goodwin corset makers claimed "world eminent doctors and surgeons recognized" their corset's "corrective powers."

A long, firmly boned corset for full figure having heavy thigh muscles.

Like model K below waist. Cut out under bust, but high enough to support diaphragm in center front.

A very practical corset, suited to the average person of medium height. It is well boned and adapted to all sizes.

Especially adapted for the woman with heavy, pendulous adbomen. Extra long model.

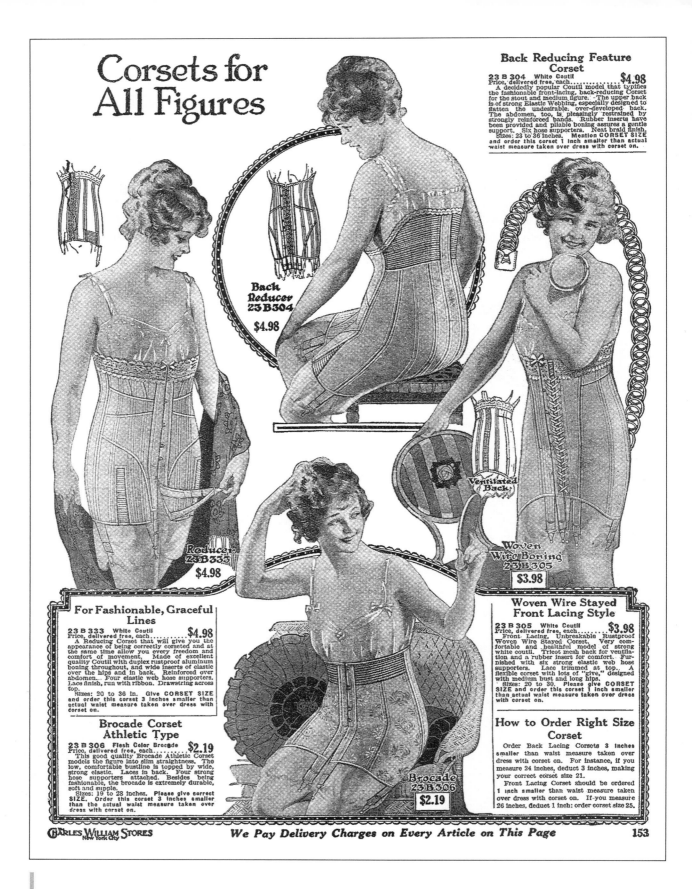

Corsets for All Figures

Back Reducing Feature Corset

23 B 304   White Coutil
Price, delivered free, each..............$4.98
A decidedly popular Coutil model that typifies the fashionable front-lacing, back-reducing Corset for the stout and medium figure. The upper back is of strong Elastic Webbing, especially designed to flatten the undesirable, over-developed back. The abdomen, too, is pleasingly restrained by strongly reinforced bands. Rubber inserts have been provided and pliable boning assures a gentle support. Six hose supporters. Neat braid finish. Sizes: 23 to 36 inches. Mention CORSET SIZE and order this corset 1 inch smaller than actual waist measure taken over dress with corset on.

Back Reducer 23 B 304 $4.98

Reducer 23 B 333 $4.98

Ventilated Back

Woven Wire Boning 23 B 305 $3.98

For Fashionable, Graceful Lines

23 B 333   White Coutil
Price, delivered free, each..............$4.98
A Reducing Corset that will give you the appearance of being correctly corseted and at the same time allow you every freedom and comfort of movement. Made of excellent quality Coutil with duplex rustproof aluminum boning throughout, and wide inserts of elastic over the hips and in back. Reinforced over abdomen. Four elastic web hose supporters. Lace finish, run with ribbon. Drawstring across top.
Sizes: 20 to 36 in. Give CORSET SIZE and order this corset 3 inches smaller than actual waist measure taken over dress with corset on.

Brocade Corset Athletic Type

23 B 306   Flesh Color Brocade
Price, delivered free, each..............$2.19
This good quality Brocade Athletic Corset models the figure into slim straightness. The low, comfortable bustline is topped by wide, strong elastic. Four strong hose supporters attached. Besides being fashionable, the brocade is extremely durable, soft and supple.
Sizes: 19 to 28 inches. Please give correct SIZE. Order this corset 3 inches smaller than the actual waist measure taken over dress with corset on.

Brocade 23 B 306 $2.19

Woven Wire Stayed Front Lacing Style

23 B 305   White Coutil
Price, delivered free, each..............$3.98
Front Lacing, Unbreakable Rustproof Woven Wire Stayed Corset. Very comfortable and healthful model of strong white coutil. Tricot mesh back for ventilation and a rubber insert for comfort. Furnished with six strong elastic web hose supporters. Lace trimmed at top. A flexible corset with lots of "give," designed with medium bust and long hips.
Sizes: 20 to 30. Please give CORSET SIZE and order this corset 1 inch smaller than actual waist measure taken over dress with corset on.

How to Order Right Size Corset

Order Back Lacing Corsets 3 inches smaller than waist measure taken over dress with corset on. For instance, if you measure 24 inches, deduct 3 inches, making your correct corset size 21.

Front Lacing Corset should be ordered 1 inch smaller than waist measure taken over dress with corset on. If you measure 26 inches, deduct 1 inch; order corset size 25.

CHARLES WILLIAM STORES New York City   *We Pay Delivery Charges on Every Article on This Page*   153

According to this 1921 *Charles William Stores* catalog, back lacing corsets fit best if ordered about 3 inches smaller than the actual waist measurement, while front lacing corsets needed to only be 1 inch smaller than the waist.

Made of "surgical elastic webbing," these 1925 corsets were designed to "encourage reducing and give the gracefully restricted figure…fashionable freedom."

A 1924 Spirella corset.

As seen in the March 1925 issue of *Ladies' Home Journal*.

The Newer Corsetry

IT really began twenty years ago, when small waists went out, and "straight fronts" came in!

From that day on, "corsets" have been gradually getting to be more and more comfortable—less and less unkind.

Now every woman insists on being straight, slender, her figure firmly yet flexibly held in. Yet she herself must be just as much at ease as if she hadn't any kind of a corset on at all!

So the corset house that has been meeting her whims from 'way back when she wanted a small waist—yes, she did, once,—is today giving her just the easy, yet firmly controlling underthings her fastidious soul demands.

There are many types of foundation garments which the House of Nemo is now offering under the new name of Nemo-flex.

The flexible girdle, guiltless of back laces, has generous panels of the soft yet firm elastic webbing which does the holding in so much better and more gently than bones did. A long brassiere tops this, to permit not the slightest "break" under your slenderest frock.

THE combination, which so cleverly combines in one a girdle with a brassiere, is another high in the favor of modern women. And Nemo-flex combinations are proportioned to fit five different types of figure. So no matter what your proportions, you can be suited in these most comfortable of all modern foundations.

Back-laces, front-laces, every type of model has undergone scrupulous revision to accord with your new needs.

The modern woman looking back on what used to be says: "I am straighter, slenderer, happier!"

The joy of corsets that will hold your figure in without heavy boning is the magic of modern times!

And the athletic, modern, sensibly-slender girl who wants next-to-nothing-at-all under her slim frocks, finds Nemo-flex light bandeaux and practically boneless little girdles exquisite in detail and flexible as her own body.

In all you will find the workmanship that has always distinguished corsetry from the House of Nemo. Shoulder straps are well made and firmly sewed on, garters are of the finest quality.

THE very elastic inserts that go into Nemo-flex girdles or brassieres are a special patent, lighter and more flexible where you want them so, firmer where the figure is heavier.

Things you never thought of—elastic shoulder straps, adjustable fastenings—all anticipated for you in these lovely Nemo-flex models.

If you would like to see them and try them on, just ask for them in any store, where you will find them at varying prices, according to the fabric. For the excellence of the foundation garments Nemo makes has long been known to every store in America. Nemo, the House of Complete Corsetry, 120 East 16th St., New York City.

A FAVORITE with the younger set, this broche and elastic girdle firmly molds the figure over the hips and allows more "give" at the waist-line. $3.50. ⸱ ⸱ In this jersey silk bandeau, just enough support for the youthful figure. $1.00. ⸱ ⸱ Ease and smoothness, girdle and brassiere in one, in this combination which so smartly carries "the lead-pencil" frock. Attractive broches. $3.00 to $22.50.

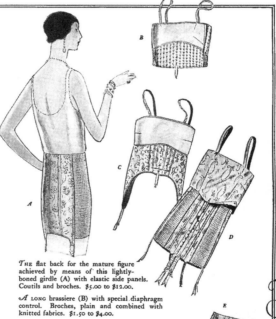

THE flat back for the mature figure achieved by means of this lightly-boned girdle (A) with elastic side panels. Coutils and broches. $5.00 to $12.00.

A LONG brassiere (B) with special diaphragm control. Broches, plain and combined with knitted fabrics. $1.50 to $4.00.

THE ample figure can be comfortably molded to slenderness by wearing, over a light girdle, this flesh-pink broche garter brassiere. (C) $3.50.

ONE of five Nemo-flex models that bring one-piece comfort to as many types of figure—this combination of girdle and brassiere (D) in prettily designed broches. $5.00 to $18.00.

THE silk covered rubber reducing girdle (E)—now as lovely as it is comfortable—appears for the first time in a dainty figured design. Lined with a fabric that absorbs perspiration. $10.75

THE figure requiring special abdominal support will find it in this girdle, which conceals the marvelously effective Wonderlift device for holding weakened muscles in their proper place. Coutils and broches. $7.50 to $15.00.

Nemo-flex
GIRDLES
BRASSIERES
COMBINATIONS

"It really began twenty years ago, when small waists went out, and 'straight fronts' came in! From that day on, 'corsets' have been gradually getting to be more and more comfortable…" As seen in a 1925 issue of *Ladies' Home Journal*.

A woman in complete 1920s underwear, from a
Barcley Custom Corsets catalog.

A typical corset from the 1920s.

A 1920s corset for a woman with a fuller figure.
The bands at the abdomen are designed to flatten.

Corsets of a wide variety of types, including "corset waists" for girls and a maternity corset. From the *M. W. Savage Co.* catalog from 1927–28.

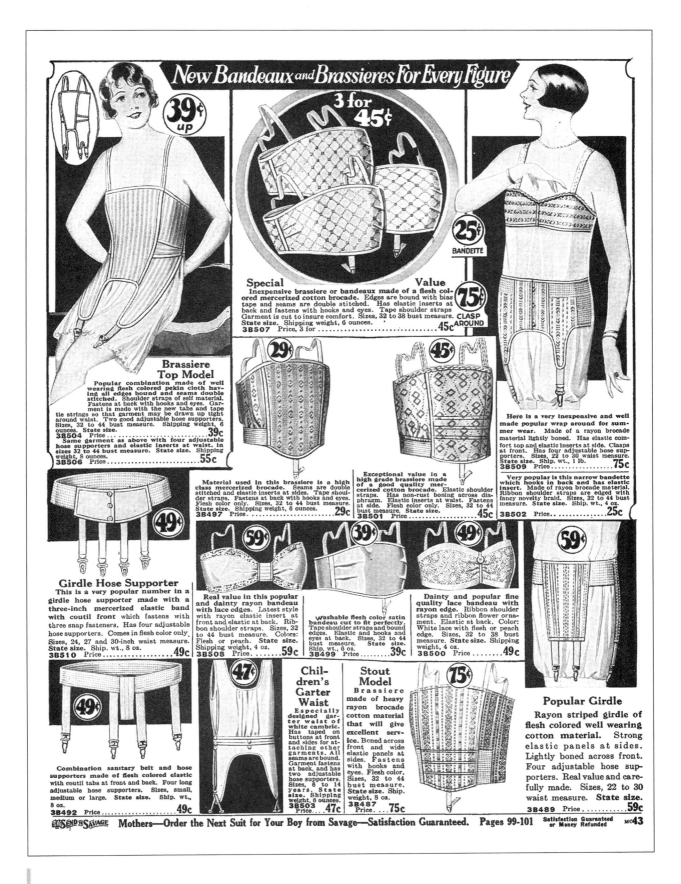

New Bandeaux and Brassieres For Every Figure

39¢ up

3 for 45¢

25¢ BANDETTE

75¢ CLASP AROUND

Brassiere Top Model

Popular combination made of well wearing flesh colored pekin cloth having all edges bound and seams double stitched. Shoulder straps of self material. Fastens at back with hooks and eyes. Garment is made with the new tabs and tape tie strings so that garment may be drawn up tight around waist. Two good adjustable hose supporters. Sizes, 32 to 44 bust measure. Shipping weight, 6 ounces. State size.
3B504 Price.........................39¢
Same garment as above with four adjustable hose supporters and elastic inserts at waist, in sizes 32 to 44 bust measure. State size. Shipping weight, 8 ounces.
3B506 Price.........................55¢

Special Value
Inexpensive brassiere or bandeaux made of a flesh colored mercerized cotton brocade. Edges are bound with bias tape and seams are double stitched. Has elastic inserts at back and fastens with hooks and eyes. Tape shoulder straps Garment is cut to insure comfort. Sizes, 32 to 38 bust measure. State size. Shipping weight, 6 ounces.
3B507 Price, 3 for..................45¢

29¢

45¢

Material used in this brassiere is a high class mercerized brocade. Seams are double stitched and elastic inserts at sides. Tape shoulder straps. Fastens at back with hooks and eyes. Flesh color only. Sizes, 32 to 44 bust measure. State size. Shipping weight, 6 ounces.
3B497 Price.........................29¢

Exceptional value in a high grade brassiere made of a good quality mercerized cotton brocade. Elastic shoulder straps. Has non-rust boning across diaphragm. Elastic inserts at side. Flesh color only. Sizes, 32 to 44 bust measure. State size.
3B501 Price.........................45¢

Here is a very inexpensive and well made popular wrap around for summer wear. Made of a rayon brocade material lightly boned. Has elastic comfort top and elastic inserts at side. Clasps at front. Has four adjustable hose supporters. Sizes, 22 to 30 waist measure. State size. Ship. wt., 1 lb.
3B509 Price.........................75¢

Very popular is this narrow bandette which hooks in back and has elastic insert. Made of rayon brocade material. Ribbon shoulder straps are edged with fancy novelty braid. Sizes, 32 to 44 bust measure. Ship. wt., 4 oz.
3B502 Price.........................25¢

49¢

Girdle Hose Supporter
This is a very popular number in a girdle hose supporter made with a three-inch mercerized elastic band with coutil front which fastens with three snap fasteners. Has four adjustable hose supporters. Comes in flesh color only. Sizes, 24, 27 and 30-inch waist measure. State size. Ship. wt., 8 oz.
3B510 Price.........................49¢

59¢

Real value in this popular and dainty rayon bandeau with lace edges. Latest style with rayon elastic insert at back. Ribbon shoulder straps. Sizes, 32 to 44 bust measure. Colors: Flesh or peach. State size. Shipping weight, 4 oz.
3B508 Price.........................59¢

39¢

Washable flesh color satin bandeau cut to fit perfectly. Tape shoulder straps and bound edges. Elastic and hooks and eyes at back. Sizes, 32 to 44 bust measure. State size. Ship. wt., 6 oz.
3B499 Price.........................39¢

49¢

Dainty and popular fine quality lace bandeau with rayon edge. Ribbon shoulder straps and ribbon flower ornament. Elastic at back. Color: White lace with flesh or peach edge. Sizes, 32 to 38 bust measure. State size. Shipping weight, 4 oz.
3B500 Price.........................49¢

59¢

49¢

Combination sanitary belt and hose supporters made of flesh colored elastic with coutil tabs at front and back. Four long adjustable hose supporters. Sizes, small, medium or large. State size. Ship. wt., 8 oz.
3B492 Price.........................49¢

47¢

Children's Garter Waist
Especially designed garter waist of white cambric. Has taped on buttons at front and sides for attaching other garments. All seams are bound. Garment fastens at back, and has two adjustable hose supporters. Sizes, 8 to 14 years. State size. Shipping weight, 6 ounces.
3B503 Price....47¢

Stout Model
Brassiere made of heavy rayon brocade cotton material that will give excellent service. Boned across front and wide elastic panels at sides. Fastens with hooks and eyes. Flesh color. Sizes, 32 to 44 bust measure. State size. Ship. weight, 8 oz.
3B487 Price....75¢

75¢

Popular Girdle
Rayon striped girdle of flesh colored well wearing cotton material. Strong elastic panels at sides. Lightly boned across front. Four adjustable hose supporters. Real value and carefully made. Sizes, 22 to 30 waist measure. State size.
3B489 Price.........................59¢

SEND IT TO SAVAGE **Mothers—Order the Next Suit for Your Boy from Savage—Satisfaction Guaranteed.** Pages 99-101 Satisfaction Guaranteed or Money Refunded MC43

When bust-supporting corsets went out of style, brassieres took over. Unlike most corsets, though, they weren't designed to uplift the bosom. They did the opposite, and flattened the breasts. Notice also the child's "waist" designed to support the stockings.

Today, most women take to loose clothes soon after discovering they are pregnant. But throughout most of history, women wore maternity corsets or girdles. These maternity girdles are from the *Charles William Stores* catalog from 1928.

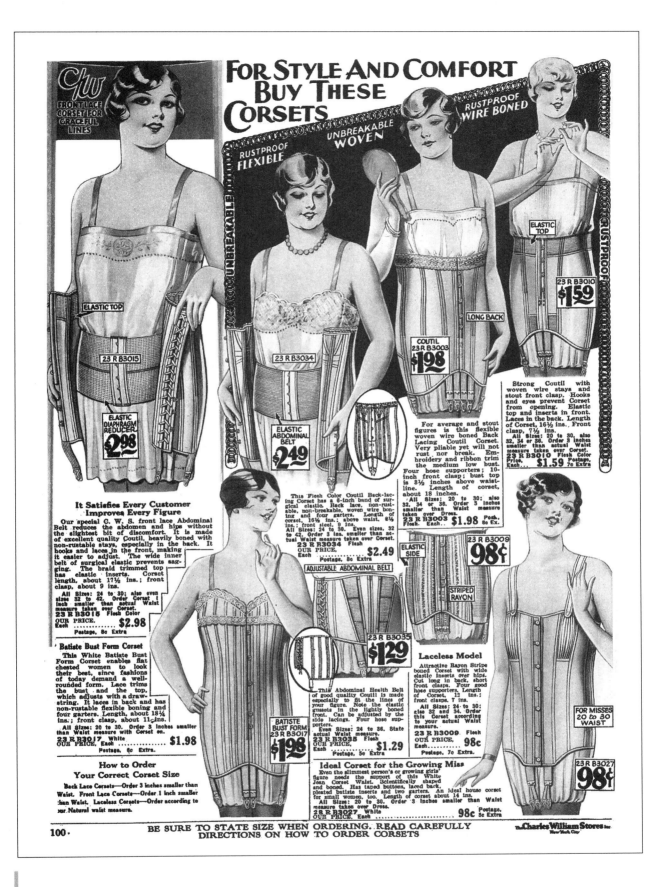

Girls and young women continued corseting in the 1920s. Like the "waists" of the Victorian era, their corsets or girdles had shoulder straps and were less compressing than models made for adults. From *Charles William Stores* catalog from 1928.

STYLED FOR EVERY FIGURE

Improves Your Figure

This low bust, heavily boned Coutil Hip and Abdominal Reducer fits smoothly. For Medium or Stout figures. It has elastic inserts over the hips in back at the braid trimmed bust, and double coutil tabs above the garters to give flatter lines. It has non-rustable stays, and four garters. Corset length, about 14½ inches; spoon front clasp, 8 inches.

All Sizes: 22 to 30; also 32, 34 or 36. Order 3 ins. smaller than waist measure taken over corset.

23 R B3016 Flesh
OUR PRICE,
Each **$1.98**
Postage, 8c Extra

Be Sure to State Your Correct Size

CW **STA-BONE REDUCING CORSET**

BACK VIEW

ELASTIC TOP

COUTIL 23 R B3016 **$1.98**

GENUINE "BELDING SATIN" 23 R B3002 **$2.49**

ELASTIC

PULLEY GARTERS

REINFORCED

FOR STOUT FIGURES

23 R B3051 **$2.98**

Special Value

Very Rich Looking

This Genuine Belding Satin Corset is backed with Flesh Color Jean. The diagonal boning in front confines any excess flesh at the abdomen. Long one-piece elastic inserts at the sides and back give ease and comfort. Four strong loop garters with pulley effect that gives with every movement of your body. Our price is very low, but we want you to see it to be convinced.

All Sizes: 24 to 30; also 32, 34 and 36. State waist measure.

23 R B3002 Flesh
OUR PRICE,
Each **$2.49**
Postage, 8c Extra

COUTIL HIP REDUCER 23 R B3011 **$1.39**

The Healthful Way to Reduce

Reducing is easy when you have the right reducer. By gradually tightening the double tabs of this Back Lacing White Coutil Corset, you can reduce your hips from one to three inches. It has non-rustable aluminum boning, medium low bust trimmed with embroidery and four garters. Corset length, about 17 inches; front clasp, about 8 inches; bust above waist, about 3½ inches high.

All Sizes: 20 to 30; also even sizes, 32 to 42. Order 3 ins. smaller than Waist measure taken over corset.

23 R B3011 White
OUR PRICE, Each ...... **$1.39** Postage, 7c Extra

DOUBLE MATERIAL **$1.29**

79¢

Fashion leaders inform us that even the very slim wear a light weight girdle these days. This one of Rayon Satin (Backed with Jean) has long back and short front making it ideal for dancing or general wear. Silk elastic over hips and four strong garters. Silk boxy in front. Light as feather but gives sufficient support to figure.

Even Sizes: 24 to 34. State Waist measure.

23 R B3004 Flesh Color
OUR PRICE,
Each .... **$1.29** Postage, 8c Extra

An ideal light girdle for the slim and average figure is offered here in a good quality Rayon Mixed material with wide elastic over the hips. The front is horizontally boned to give the figure flat lines. Ideal for the athletic woman. The growing girl will also find this girdle very comfortable for moulding her figure. Very inexpensive too.

Even Sizes: 24 to 34 inches. State Actual Waist measure.

23 R B3008 Flesh
OUR PRICE,
Each .... **79¢** Postage, 5c Extra

FOR STOUT WOMEN

ELASTIC TOP

23 R B3019 **$1.98**

COUTIL

ELASTIC ABDOMINAL BELT

Our Well-Known C/W "Sta-Boned" Reducing Corset

This Coutil Corset for the Stout Woman is especially constructed so that the boning will not poke out and bruise the fleshy part of the abdomen. It is strongly reenforced in front to prevent the clasp from wearing through and the garters are riveted on. The elastic in the backs keeps the corset from riding up and pulls the figure in comfortably. It is made of a very fine quality Coutil with elastic side and back inserts which are riveted so that they cannot possibly pull out. Small elastic gussets in front to insure comfort. Length of corset about 17 ins. Spoon front clasp 9½ ins. long. Height of Bust above waist, 2½ ins. This model has back lacing. Any woman can improve her figure by wearing this well-made reducing corset. Specially designed so that the figure is gradually reduced comfortably and healthfully. Our price is very low for this quality.

All Sizes: 24 to 30; also even sizes 32 to 44. Order this corset three inches smaller than waist measure over dress.

23 R B3051 Flesh Color
OUR PRICE, Each .... **$2.98** Postage, 10c Extra

A Special Value In a Back Lace Model Medium and Stout Figures

We are offering this special value to the thousands of women throughout the country who need a good substantial corset at a reasonable price. This one in particular is well made of good quality Flesh Color Coutil with inner belt of the coutil and wide surgical elastic webbing. The proportions are especially suited to the medium and stout woman. Certainly you wouldn't want a better fitting corset, for it fits smoothly over the hips. Comfort features of the corset section are the short front steels, the wide front reenforcement and the elastic inserts at the top and in back. Corset length, abt. 17 ins.; front clasp, abt. 7½ ins.

All Sizes: 24 to 30. Also Sizes 32, 34 and 36. Order 3 ins. smaller than actual Waist measure taken over corset. State Corset Size.

23 R B3019 Flesh Color
OUR PRICE,
Each .... **$1.98** Postage, 8c Extra

The *Charles William Stores* 1928 catalog claimed girdles were "the healthy way to reduce" the figure. "By gradually tightening" some girdles, "you can reduce your hips from one to three inches."

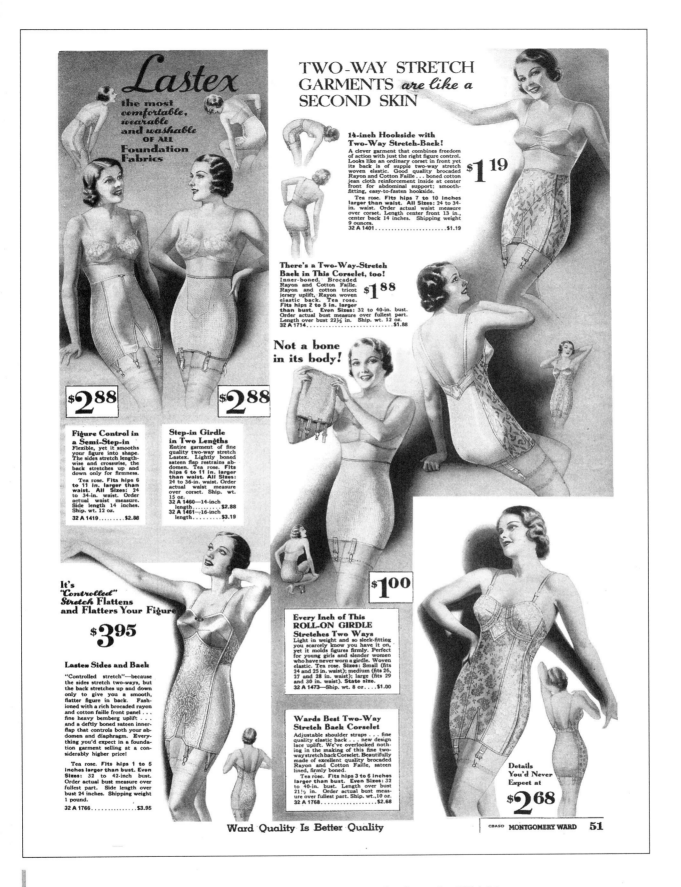

Notice how extreme flexibility was emphasized for these girdles from the 1934 *Montgomery Ward* catalog. Girdle makers and sellers often emphasized undergarments with "not a bone in its body," but many girdles still contained feather boning or spiral steels.

FIRM SUPPORT *without an* **INNER BELT**

$1.39

Our Lowest Priced Corselet with the Two Way Stretch Back

A Corselet that molds your figure into unbroken lines without curtailing your freedom of action because of its firm yet flexible two-way stretch elastic back. Good brocaded rayon and cotton Faille . . . entire back of rayon woven elastic . . . boned cotton jean cloth flap fashioned into the inside to restrain diaphragm and abdomen. All these fine details of construction at a typical low Ward price!

Tea rose. Fits hips 2 to 5 inches larger than bust. Even Sizes: 32 to 40-inch bust. Length over bust 21 inches. Order actual bust measure over fullest part. Shipping weight 10 ounces.
32 A 1716 . . . .$1.39

$1.39

DIAB CONTROL does the trick
. . . and it's really **LOW PRICED**

$1.19

Diab control restrains both diaphragm and abdomen. Of rayon figured cotton Poplin, double faced rayon elastic sides, well boned.

Tea rose. Fits hips 2 to 5 in. larger than bust. Even Sizes: 32 to 46-inch bust. Order actual bust measure over fullest part. Length over bust 22½ inches. Shipping weight 12 ounces.
32 A 1735. . . . .$1.19

Exceptionally FINE QUALITY

$2.68

Rich brocaded rayon and cotton Faille with fine rayon woven elastic. Firmly boned Coutil Diab control. Rayon Tricot Jersey uplift.

Tea rose. Fits hips 3 to 6 in. larger than bust. Even Sizes: 34 to 46-in. bust. Order actual bust measure over fullest part. Length over bust 23 inches. Shipping weight 1 pound.
32 A 1804. . . . .$2.68

A Last Year's BEST SELLER Improved in Quality!

Finer fitting . . . fashioned of better quality brocaded rayon and cotton Faille. Smart lace uplift . . . supple elastic side sections . . . well boned for ample support. An excellent value.

Tea rose. Fits hips 2 to 5 inches larger than bust. Even Sizes: 32 to 42-inch bust. Order actual bust measure over fullest part. Length over bust 21 inches. Shipping weight 10 ounces.
32 A 1795. . . . . . .$1.39

Our LOWEST PRICED Corselet . . . Perfect for Slender Figures!

If you want to feel trim but not corseted, here's your Corselet. Rayon figured cotton Poplin, elastic side inserts, diaphragm lightly boned.

Flesh pink. Fits hips 2 to 5 in. larger than bust. Even Sizes: 32 to 44-in. bust. Order actual bust measure over fullest part. Length over bust 19 inches. Shipping weight 8 oz.
32 A 1648. . . . . .89c

89c

Waistline Models for FIRM ABDOMINAL SUPPORT

Clasp-arounds for those smooth **BACK LINES**

You can always adjust a Back Lace to fit!

$1.00 **High Bust Model**
Popular because it keeps excess waistline flesh in place. Sturdy cotton Jean Cloth . . . well boned for firm hip control. Tea rose. Fits hips 9 to 12 in. larger than waist. Sizes: 24 to 36-in. waist. Order size 2 in. smaller than actual waist measure over corset. Height above waist in back 3 in.; skirt length 13 inches.
32 A 1400—Shipping weight 1 pound. $1.00

Wards DUROLASTIC in Three Lengths
Brocaded rayon and cotton Faille front, elastic sides, back.

$1.88

12-Inch

Tea rose. Fits hips 8 to 12 in. larger than waist. Order actual waist measure taken over corset. Shipping weight, each, 1 pound 2 ounces.
32 A 1623—12-in. length. All Sizes: 26 to 36 inch waist. $1.88
32 A 1625—14-in. length. All Sizes: 26 to 36 in.; also 38 and 40 in. waist. . . . $2.19
32 A 1627—16-in. length. All Sizes: 26 to 36; also 38 and 40 inch waist. $2.39

14-Inch Length for Light Support
A youthful Girdle that offers average figures just the right amount of comfortable restraint. Brocaded rayon and cotton Faille, with snug elastic band at top to nip in your waist and at sides to mold your hips . . . gives those smooth lines you're anxious to acquire.

$1.00

Tea rose. Fits hips 6 to 10 in. larger than waist. All Sizes: 24 to 36-inch waist. Order actual waist measure. Shipping weight 10 ounces.
32 A 1536 . . . .$1.00

$1.00

$1.39

Firmly Boned
Rayon figured cotton Poplin. Well reinforced. Rayon elastic band at top both front and sides.
Tea rose. Fits hips 9 to 13 in. larger than waist. All Sizes: 24 to 36-in. waist. Order size 2 inches smaller than waist measure over corset. Back 14¾ in. long. Ship. wt. 13 oz.
32 AX 1544. . . . .$1.00

Waistline Model
Cotton Jean Cloth. Double abdominal reinforcement of self-fabric and elastic. Well-boned.
Tea rose. Fits hips 9 to 14 in. larger than waist. All Sizes: 24 to 36-in. waist. Order size 2 in. smaller than actual waist measure. Back length 16 in. Ship. wt. $1.39
32 A 1560 . . . .$1.39

$1.59

Reinforced Across the Front
A better quality brocaded rayon and cotton Faille. Well boned for smooth line in front and firm support in back. Elastic band at waist. Tea rose. Fits hips 9 to 12 in. larger than waist. Order size 2 in. smaller than actual waist measure over corset. Length center back 15 in. Shipping wt. 14 oz.
32 A 1520 . . . .$1.59

It Costs You Less When You Buy by Mail

The simpler styles in the top row of this *Montgomery Ward* catalog page look very much like modern day shape wear, available at any department store.

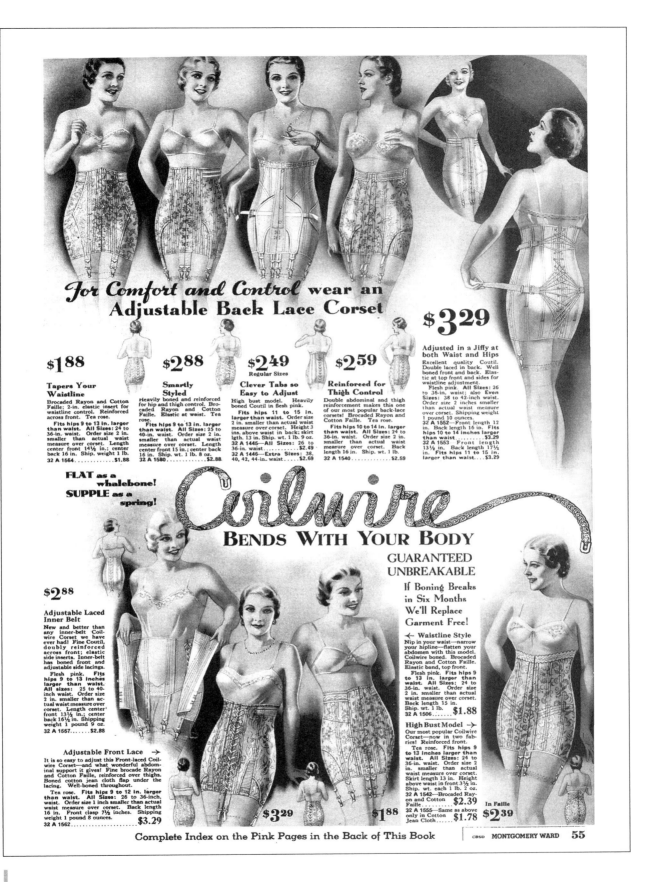

For Comfort and Control wear an Adjustable Back Lace Corset

$3.29

Adjusted in a Jiffy at both Waist and Hips
Excellent quality Coutil. Double laced in back. Well boned front and back. Elastic at top front and sides for waistline adjustment.
Flesh pink. All Sizes: 26 to 36-in. waist; also Even Sizes: 38 to 42-inch waist. Order size 2 inches smaller than actual waist measure over corset. Shipping weight 1 pound 10 ounces.
32 A 1552—Front length 12 in. Back length 16 in. Fits hips 10 to 14 inches larger than actual waist.....$3.29
32 A 1553—Front length 13½ in. Back length 17½ in. Fits hips 11 to 15 in. larger than waist.....$3.29

$1.88

Tapers Your Waistline
Brocaded Rayon and Cotton Faille; 2-in. elastic insert for waistline control. Reinforced across front. Tea rose.
Fits hips 9 to 13 in. larger than waist. All Sizes: 24 to 36-in. waist. Order size 2 in. smaller than actual waist measure over corset. Length center front 14½ in.; center back 16 in. Ship. weight 1 lb.
32 A 1564.............$1.88

$2.88

Smartly Styled
Heavily boned and reinforced for hip and thigh control. Brocaded Rayon and Cotton Faille. Elastic at waist. Tea rose.
Fits hips 9 to 13 in. larger than waist. All Sizes: 25 to 40-in. waist. Order size 2 in. smaller than actual waist measure over corset. Length center front 15 in.; center back 16 in. Ship. wt. 1 lb. 8 oz.
32 A 1580.............$2.88

$2.49
Regular Sizes

Clever Tabs so Easy to Adjust
High bust model. Heavily boned Coutil in flesh pink.
Fits hips 11 to 15 in. larger than waist. Order size 2 in. smaller than actual waist measure over corset. Height 3 ins. above waist in back; skirt lgth. 13 in. Ship. wt. 1 lb. 9 oz.
32 A 1445—All Sizes: 26 to 36-in. waist.........$2.49
32 A 1446—Extra Sizes: 38, 40, 42, 44-in. waist.....$2.69

$2.59

Reinforced for Thigh Control
Double abdominal and thigh reinforcement makes this one of our most popular back-lace corsets! Brocaded Rayon and Cotton Faille. Tea rose.
Fits hips 10 to 14 in. larger than waist. All Sizes: 24 to 36-in. waist. Order size 2 in. smaller than actual waist measure over corset. Back length 16 in. Ship. wt. 1 lb.
32 A 1540.............$2.59

FLAT as a whalebone!
SUPPLE as a spring!

Coilwire
BENDS WITH YOUR BODY

GUARANTEED UNBREAKABLE

If Boning Breaks in Six Months We'll Replace Garment Free!

$2.88

Adjustable Laced Inner Belt
New and better than any inner-belt Coilwire Corset we have ever had! Fine Coutil, doubly reinforced across front; elastic side inserts. Inner-belt has boned front and adjustable side lacings.
Flesh pink. Fits hips 9 to 13 inches larger than waist. All sizes: 25 to 40-inch waist. Order size 2 in. smaller than actual waist measure over corset. Length center front 13½ in.; center back 16½ in. Shipping weight 1 pound 9 oz.
32 A 1557......$2.88

Adjustable Front Lace →
It is so easy to adjust this Front-laced Coilwire Corset—and what wonderful abdominal support it gives! Fine brocade Rayon and Cotton Faille, reinforced over thighs. Boned cotton jean cloth flap under the lacing. Well-boned throughout.
Tea rose. Fits hips 9 to 12 in. larger than waist. All Sizes: 26 to 36-inch. waist. Order size 1 inch smaller than actual waist measure over corset. Back length 16 in. Front clasp 7½ inches. Shipping weight 1 pound 8 ounces.
32 A 1562......................$3.29

$3.29

$1.88

← Waistline Style
Nip in your waist—narrow your hipline—flatten your abdomen with this model. Coilwire boned. Brocaded Rayon and Cotton Faille. Elastic band, top front.
Flesh pink. Fits hips 9 to 13 in. larger than waist. All Sizes: 24 to 36-in. waist. Order size 2 in. smaller than actual waist measure over corset. Back length 15 in. Ship. wt. 1 lb.
32 A 1506.......$1.88

High Bust Model →
Our most popular Coilwire Corset—now in two fabrics! Reinforced front.
Tea rose. Fits hips 9 to 13 inches larger than waist. All Sizes: 24 to 36-in. waist. Order size 2 in. smaller than actual waist measure over corset. Skirt length 13 in. Height above waist in front 3½ in.
32 A 1542—Brocaded Rayon and Cotton Faille.....$2.39
32 A 1555—Same as above only in Cotton Jean Cloth.....$1.78

$2.39
In Faille

Complete Index on the Pink Pages in the Back of This Book

Boned girdles, guaranteed to not break within 6 months.

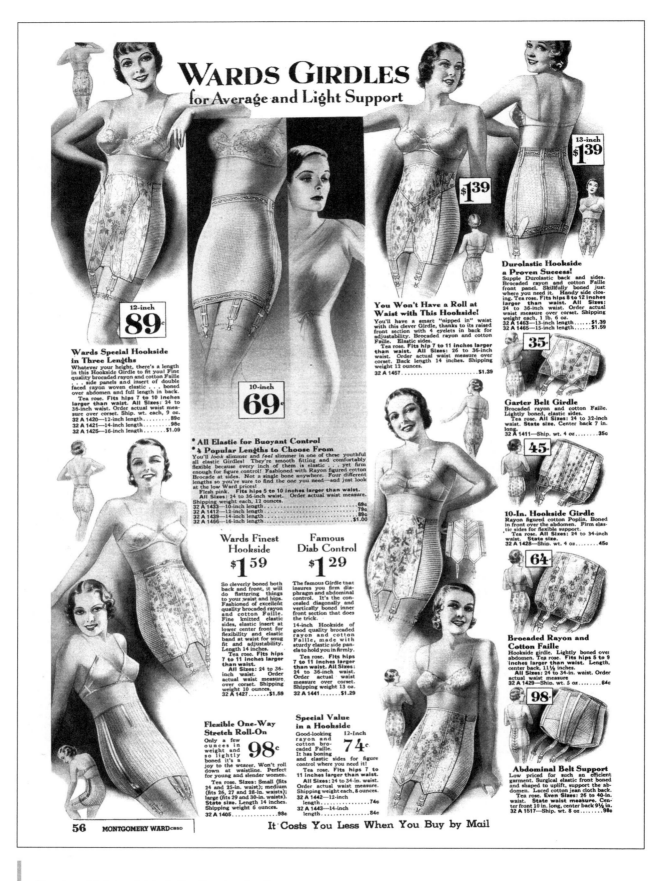

WARDS GIRDLES
for Average and Light Support

12-inch 89c

10-inch 69c

$1.39

13-inch $1.39

$1.39

35c

45c

64c

98c

Wards Special Hookside in Three Lengths
Whatever your height, there's a length in this Hookside Girdle to fit you! Fine quality brocaded rayon and cotton Faille . . . side panels and insert of double faced rayon woven elastic . . . boned over abdomen and full length in back.
Tea rose. Fits hips 7 to 10 inches larger than waist. All Sizes: 24 to 36-inch waist. Order actual waist measure over corset. Ship. wt. each, 9 oz.
32 A 1420—12-inch length........89c
32 A 1421—14-inch length........98c
32 A 1425—16-inch length......$1.09

* All Elastic for Buoyant Control
4 Popular Lengths to Choose From
You'll *look* slimmer and *feel* slimmer in one of these youthful all elastic Girdles! They're smooth fitting and comfortably flexible because every inch of them is elastic . . . yet firm enough for figure control! Fashioned with Rayon figured cotton Brocade at sides. Not a single bone anywhere. Four different lengths so you're sure to find the one you need—and just look at the low Ward prices!
Flesh pink. Fits hips 5 to 10 inches larger than waist.
All Sizes: 24 to 36-inch waist. Order actual waist measure. Shipping weight each, 12 ounces.
32 A 1433—10-inch length.........................69c
32 A 1412—12-inch length.........................79c
32 A 1439—14-inch length.........................89c
32 A 1456—16-inch length.........................$1.00

Wards Finest Hookside $1.59
So cleverly boned both back and front, it will do flattering things to your waist and hips. Fashioned of excellent quality brocaded rayon and cotton Faille. Fine knitted elastic sides, elastic insert at lower center front for flexibility and elastic band at waist for snug fit and adjustability. Length 14 inches.
Tea rose. Fits hips 7 to 11 inches larger than waist.
All Sizes: 24 to 36-inch waist. Order actual waist measure over corset. Shipping weight 10 ounces.
32 A 1427......$1.59

Famous Diab Control $1.29
The famous Girdle that insures you firm diaphragm and abdominal control. It's the concealed diagonally and vertically boned inner front section that does the trick.
14-inch Hookside of good quality brocaded rayon and cotton Faille, made with sturdy elastic side panels to hold you in firmly.
Tea rose. Fits hips 7 to 11 inches larger than waist. All Sizes: 24 to 36-inch waist. Order actual waist measure over corset. Shipping weight 13 oz.
32 A 1441......$1.29

You Won't Have a Roll at Waist with This Hookside!
You'll have a smart "nipped in" waist with this clever Girdle, thanks to its raised front section with 4 eyelets in back for adjustability. Brocaded rayon and cotton Faille. Elastic sides.
Tea rose. Fits hips 7 to 11 inches larger than waist. All Sizes: 26 to 36-inch waist. Order actual waist measure over corset. Back length 14 inches. Shipping weight 12 ounces.
32 A 1457.......................$1.39

Durolastic Hookside a Proven Success!
Supple Durolastic back and sides. Brocaded rayon and cotton Faille front panel. Skillfully boned just where you need it. Handy side closing. Tea rose. Fits hips 8 to 12 inches larger than waist. All Sizes: 24 to 36-inch waist. Order actual waist measure over corset. Shipping weight each, 1 lb. 6 oz.
32 A 1463—13-inch length.....$1.39
32 A 1465—15-inch length.....$1.59

Garter Belt Girdle
Brocaded rayon and cotton Faille. Lightly boned, elastic sides.
Tea rose. All Sizes: 24 to 32-inch waist. State size. Center back 7 in. long.
32 A 1411—Ship. wt. 4 oz....35c

10-In. Hookside Girdle
Rayon figured cotton Poplin. Boned in front over the abdomen. Firm elastic sides for flexible support.
Tea rose. All Sizes: 24 to 34-inch waist. State size.
32 A 1428—Ship. wt. 4 oz....45c

Brocaded Rayon and Cotton Faille
Hookside girdle. Lightly boned over abdomen. Tea rose. Fits hips 5 to 9 inches larger than waist. Length, center back, 11½ inches.
All Sizes: 24 to 34-in. waist. Order actual waist measure
32 A 1429—Ship. wt. 5 oz.......64c

Flexible One-Way Stretch Roll-On 98c
Only a few ounces in weight and so lightly boned it's a joy to the wearer. Won't roll down at waistline. Perfect for young and slender women. Ten rose. Sizes: Small (fits 24 and 25-in. waist); medium (fits 26, 27 and 28-in. waists); large (fits 29 and 30-in. waists). State size. Length 14 inches. Shipping weight 6 ounces.
32 A 1405.............98c

Special Value in a Hookside 74c 12-inch
Good-looking rayon and cotton brocaded Faille. It has boning and elastic sides for figure control where you need it!
Tea rose. Fits hips 7 to 11 inches larger than waist. All Sizes: 24 to 34-in. waist. Order actual waist measure. Shipping weight each, 8 ounces.
32 A 1442—12-inch length...............74c
32 A 1443—14-inch length...............84c

Abdominal Belt Support
Low priced for such an efficient garment. Surgical elastic front boned and shaped to uplift, support the abdomen. Laced cotton jean cloth back. Tea rose. Even Sizes: 26 to 40-in. waist. State waist measure. Center front 10 in. long, center back 9½ in.
32 A 1517—Ship. wt. 8 oz.......98c

It Costs You Less When You Buy by Mail

Short and lightweight girdles for slender figures.

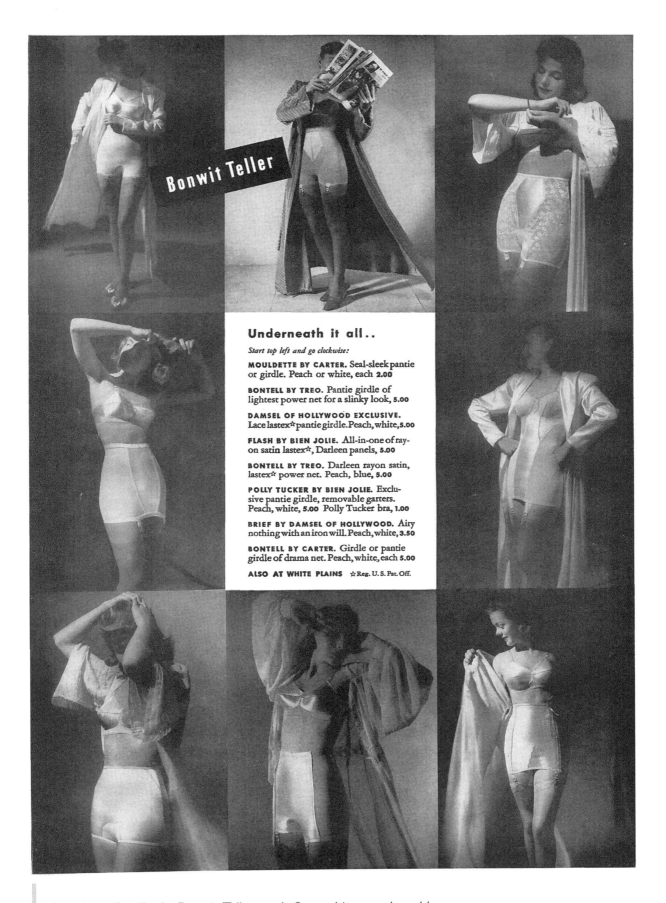

Bonwit Teller

Underneath it all..

Start top left and go clockwise:

MOULDETTE BY CARTER. Seal-sleek pantie or girdle. Peach or white, each **2.00**

BONTELL BY TREO. Pantie girdle of lightest power net for a slinky look, **5.00**

DAMSEL OF HOLLYWOOD EXCLUSIVE. Lace lastex☆ pantie girdle. Peach, white, **5.00**

FLASH BY BIEN JOLIE. All-in-one of rayon satin lastex☆, Darleen panels, **5.00**

BONTELL BY TREO. Darleen rayon satin, lastex☆ power net. Peach, blue, **5.00**

POLLY TUCKER BY BIEN JOLIE. Exclusive pantie girdle, removable garters. Peach, white, **5.00** Polly Tucker bra, **1.00**

BRIEF BY DAMSEL OF HOLLYWOOD. Airy nothing with an iron will. Peach, white, **3.50**

BONTELL BY CARTER. Girdle or pantie girdle of drama net. Peach, white, each **5.00**

ALSO AT WHITE PLAINS   ☆Reg. U.S. Pat. Off.

A variety of girdles by Bonwit Teller, made from white, peach, or blue power net and Lastex, selling for $2 to $5 in 1941.

WARNER'S LE GANT* STA-UP-TOP*

WON'T ROLL OVER

Don't let your figure go to seed!

...keep your chassis streamlined with a Warner's Le Gant! Here's a pantie-girdle that meets all specifications: it's *comfortable*—it controls bulges —the Sta-Up-Top won't flop over at your waistline—it fits your budget, too! *And the bra is grand with sweaters!*

Le Gant pantie-girdles $5 and up
(Warnerettes for as little as $2!)
The bra is only $1!

Write for illustrated booklet "Recipes for Figure Beauty".
The Warner Brothers Company, 200 Madison Avenue, New York, N. Y.
In Canada: Parision Corset Mfg. Co., Quebec.
*Reg. U. S. Pat. Off.   Pat. No. 2,136,742.

With a special "Sta-Up-Top" of wide elastic, this 1941 Warner girdle promised to solve a common problem: Roll down.

*"Variation" brassiere gives *average* bosoms a marked line-of-separation —$1.00, 1.50, 2.00 and up; shown with *"Curtsy" two-way-stretch Pantie Girdle No. 1526 —$2.00

MAIDEN FORM helps you to Get your ‡B.S. in Figures!

Yes, in the right foundations by Maiden Form, you're sure of your B. S.— "Better Silhouette," that important extra-curricula degree so necessary to social and scholastic success! You'll feel better and look better in the garments Maiden Form created especially for your figure-type. So, start your new semester with a complete wardrobe of Maiden Form's individualized brassieres and girdles. Or, if you prefer one-piece foundations ask for *"Once-Overs" made with Maiden Form's own brassiere tops.

‡ B.S.— "Better Silhouette"

"Once-Over" with two-way-stretch body section and "Allegro" brassiere top for smart "outlift" as well as "uplift." The brassiere has adjustable back and shoulder straps, to give fit to a fraction-of-an-inch — $3.50

AT ALL LEADING STORES

Maiden Form

LOOK FOR THIS TRADE-MARK ON
BRASSIERES
GIRDLES · "ONCE-OVERS" *Reg. U. S. Pat. Off.
"There is a Maiden Form for Every Type of Figure!"

Maiden Form was founded in 1922, and always promoted womanly figures. By the time fashion caught up with Maiden Form designers, the company was a leader in bras and girdles. This ad appeared in the August 1941 issue of *Harper's Bazaar*.

Rear Guard

WHAT TO DO IN AN AIR RAID

...that's war-talk for wonderful Jantzen panty-girdles that bring down the rear, trim the ribs, belittle the waist, smooth the tummy, streamline the hips...put you at ease in your slacks and uniforms. They stay up at the top, down at the bottom without pinching, poking, binding or twisting. They're sheer and sure...cool and comfortable...as flexible as Jantzen swim suits...wash as easily as your skin...5.00 to 7.50. Other Jantzen foundations 2.95 to 10.00 at all leading stores.

JANTZEN FOUNDATION DIVISION • DOVER, N. J.

Jantzen THE FOUNDATION OF NATURAL BEAUTY

Jantzen, a maker of swimsuits since the teens, produced many girdles in the 1940s. This 1942 ad plays heavy on WWII and the "slacks and uniforms" women sometimes wore at that time.

Gossard, a Victorian favorite, was still advertising corsets and girdles in 1942.

Hickory "panties" from 1945, designed to "gently but firmly mold our figure yet give you complete and unrestricted comfort."

By the 40s, zippers were often found in women's clothing in general, and corsets in particular. This corset appeared in the October 1947 issue of *Charm*.

Silhouette for Summer

...day
into
evening

QUITE a sensation, the Flexnit label in underneath fashions — where the streamlining of your summer outline starts. With a Flexnit Foundation, you'll rejoice in the figure you cut in your business clothes—and revel in the comfort and freedom with which that dramatic smoothness is achieved. It's a comfort that carries you through working hours fresh for the enchantment of mid-summer evenings . . . a freedom that keeps you in good form later in your glamour togs—in spirit as well as in figure!

It's the better shops and stores that carry Flexnit Foundations. But please be patient if you have to wait a little.

ALL-IN-ONES • GIRDLES • PANTIE-GIRDLES
PANTIES • GARTER BELTS • HOSE-SUPPORTERS

Look for This Label

FLEXNIT

FOUNDATIONS

Shown: Flexnit Girdle with Talon slide-fastener closing, four all-elastic garters, fagot-stitched front panel, up-and-down stretch rayon satin back panel, two-way stretch side sections.

F L E X N I T, *200 Madison Avenue, New York 16, New York*

A 1945 Flexnit ad featuring a girdle with a zipper closing, made of stretch rayon satin.

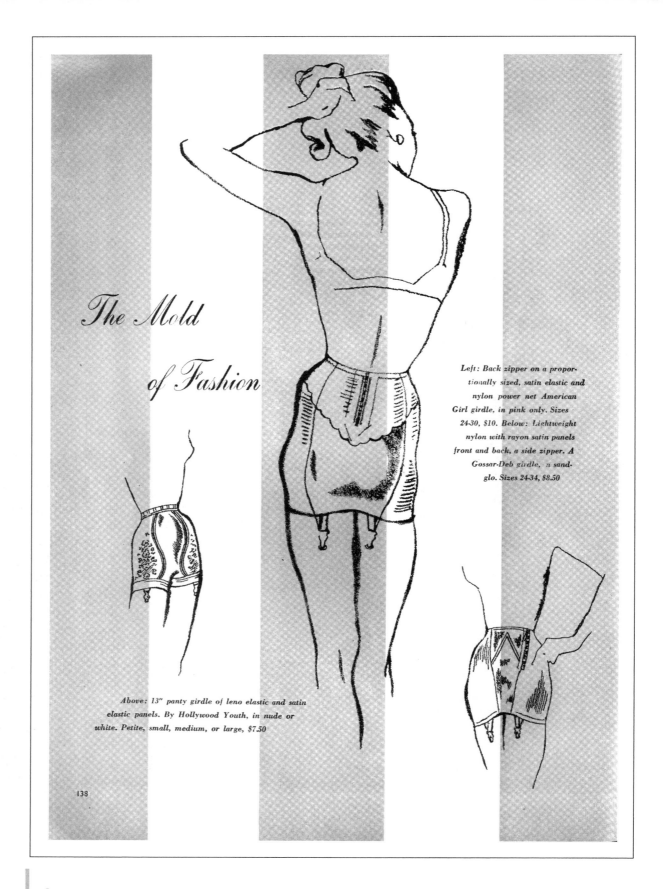

The Mold
of Fashion

Left: Back zipper on a proportionally sized, satin elastic and nylon power net American Girl girdle, in pink only. Sizes 24-30, $10. Below: Lightweight nylon with rayon satin panels front and back, a side zipper. A Gossar-Deb girdle, a sand-glo. Sizes 24-34, $8.50

Above: 13" panty girdle of leno elastic and satin elastic panels. By Hollywood Youth, in nude or white. Petite, small, medium, or large, $7.50

138

Girdles with legs were called "panty girdles." Most girdles of this time period were now made with nylon netting and elastic. These girdles came in white, pinks, or nude and were featured in a 1947 issue of *Charm.*

hold
that
line
with **Cupid** "your closest friend"

You'll want to buy all the
glamorous new fashions in sight the
moment you slip into a CUPID
girdle or panty girdle! Your figure will look . . .
divine! Lightweight, freedom-
loving, wonderful in action
. . . Cupid Foundations are
1.25 to 7.50.

style
205
about
$3.50

Send for
free booklet
"A Lovelier You"

The figure beauty
of the Cupid girl . . .
yours with fabulous
Cupid Controllers

At your favorite store, or write

CUPID FOUNDATIONS, INC.
5 East 35th Street, New York 16.

This Cupid girdle from 1947 received the
Good Housekeeping Seal of Approval.

Restrain Yourself . . .
in *Real-form*

Don't reach for that
cookie, cookie, but do reach
for a Real-form Girdle or Panty Girdle!
These super smoothers are Raschel-Knitted,
fashioned to fit of 2-way stretch Lastex.
Guaranteed non-run. With removable
crotch. Also with panels. $5.
Write for Free Illustrated Booklet, Dept. 4-C

REAL-FORM GIRDLE CO. • 358 FIFTH AVE., NEW YORK 1, N. Y.

"Don't reach for that cookie, cookie, but do reach
for a Real-form Girdle or Panty Girdle!" Made
from knitted Lastex, this girdle was $5 in 1947.

Amazing Free Trial Offer!

Here's the new 2-way stretch everyone is talking
about . . . covered with that wonder-material DuPont
Nylon! You'll be thrilled by this pre-shrunk fabric
that washes and dries so miraculously fast. And
you'll be enchanted by the form-hug design that
gently restrains embarrassing bulges.
Two lovely styles . . . panty girdle with
removable snap-button crotch and removable garter straps, or the beautifully
styled regular type. Colors: Nude, White,
Blue and Black.

WASHES "LIKE A DREAM"

Examine and wear this soft, bargain in 2-way-stretch
comfortable, slenderizing NY- girdles you have ever worn,
LON girdle for ten days with- or it costs you absolutely
out risk. You must be con- nothing. Send no money . . .
vinced that this is the biggest just the coupon NOW!

NEW NYLON
2-WAY STRETCH
GIRDLE

ENJOY
THESE
AMAZING
FEATURES
• Nylon Fabric
• Pre-Shrunk
• Dries in
  Minutes
• Form-hug
  Design
• Low Cost
• 2 thrilling
  Styles

ANNETTE FASHIONS CO., Dept. L102
45 E. 17 St., New York 3, N. Y.
☐ Rush_____NYLON girdles ☐ Panty ☐ Regular.
I will pay postman only $3.98 each ($4.98 for waist sizes 31-30.)
plus postage. Send_____extra crotches at 49c each C.O.D.
plus postage. If not completely satisfied I may return within 10
days for full purchase price refund.
☐ Small 23-25. ☐ Medium 26-27. ☐ Large 28-30.
☐ X Large 31-33. ☐XX Large 34-36. ☐ XXX Large 37-39.
Check color: ☐ Nude ☐ White ☐ Blue ☐ Black
☐ Check here if you enclose money now. We pay postage. Same
refund guarantee.

Name_____
Address_____
City_____Zone_____State_____

Annette Fashions advertised this nylon,
2-way stretch girdle in 1947.

Gossar-Deb STEP-IN *Extravagantly feminine — is the word for you. Infinitesimal*
of waist . . . longer of mid-riff . . . higher of bosom . . . gently curving of hipline. Gossard achieved, with Talon
fastened, all Nylon step-in (satin paneled, satin leno elastic); Nylon sheer bra.

the **Gossard** *line of beauty*

Designed to shrink the waist and lengthen the
midriff, Gossard sold this nylon girdle in 1947.

Magnetic new glamor...with *Life*

No other bra and girdle can give you this glamorous
figure line, above the waist *and* below. Because *only* Life Bra
and Life Girdle are so cleverly tailored to fit and work
together, for enticing curve-control with supple comfort.
No wonder more women wear these Formfit creations
than any other underfashions. Life Bras
$1.25 to $3.50. Life Girdles $7.50 up. Be fitted
today. At better stores everywhere.

A Formfit CREATION

MADE ONLY BY THE FORMFIT COMPANY, CHICAGO, NEW YORK

In your size... *your correct length*

Warner's go any length to please you. Now you
can choose from *short, medium, long* or *extra long*
lengths ... one just right for you. Only Warner's
make Half-Size corselettes, like the one shown
here. They're long on comfort, if you're short-
waisted.

.... *your correct hip size*

You don't mind taking a trimming where hips
are concerned. But a girdle that's *too small* at
the hips causes unlovely thigh bulges. One that's
too wide ripples down the sides. For the smoothest
trimming ever, Warner's girdles and corselettes
are hip-sized; *straight, average* and *full.*

.... *your choice of control*

You'll be hugged but never squeezed in your
Warner's ... whether you choose the easy-does-it
control of light, mesh elastics or the stronger
control of tightly woven elastics. Warner's corselettes are ABC cup-sized, too, just like all famous-
for-fitting Warner's bras.

"No wonder more women wear these
Formfit creations than any other
underfashions" a 1947 Formfit ad proclaimed.

From a 1949 ad, which stressed that
Warner girdles came in "short, medium,
long and extra long" lengths.

At Last!...the Wonder Girdle!

Ah!—what a wonderful feeling of comfort—what a sigh of relief! the instant you put on FIRMASTYLE . . . the famous 3-way control girdle! Preferred by thousands of fashion-conscious women for its *perfect* fit. Weighs only 6½ ounces yet meticulously designed to give heavenly lines to heavier figures. Holds and supports firmly but gently. FIRMASTYLE flattens tummy, curves hips and diminishes waist from 1 to 2 inches. 3 to 6 inch spread at bottom for comfortable sitting.

• Proportioned to 6 figure lengths. Made of Skinner's fine satin nylon and nylon leno elastic. At leading stores, or write us for name of store nearest you and copy of "Tips on How to Achieve Figure Charm." Note: FIRMASTYLE is approved by the Journal of the AMA.

Guaranteed by Good Housekeeping

PRECIZE Foundations
14 East 32nd St.
New York 1, N. Y.

Weighing just 6½ ounces, 1949's Firmastyle girdle was supposed to give "heavenly lines to heavier figures."

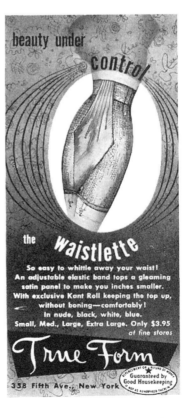

"YOU LOOK LOVELIER— *Naturally*"

Beautiful, shapely, youthful—
just the way nature intended—
that's the picture of you wearing
a NATURFLEX bra and girdle.
Your figure is molded into
lovelier lines than you would have
dreamed possible—yet so naturally—
so artfully—this perfection
seems your very own!

Bras 69c to $1.00 & $1.19 (AA, A, B & C cups)
Girdles from $1.00 to $1.98

AT YOUR FAVORITE CHAIN AND VARIETY STORE

AS NATIONALLY ADVERTISED
Naturflex PRODUCTS
Guaranteed by Good Housekeeping
LOOK FOR THIS LABEL

Naturflex
GIRDLES & BRAS
53 West 23rd St., N.Y. 10, N.Y.

Styled for the discriminating.
Priced for the budget-minded.

This Naturflex girdle sold for $1 to $1.98 in 1949.

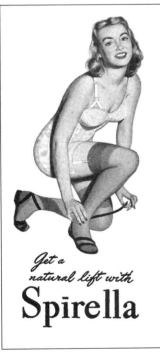

You'll find new corset comfort with Spirella

BUT comfort isn't all my new Spirella gives. Now my figure gets proper support. The perpetual tiredness that spoiled my fun is gone. I look and feel younger with more pep than I've had in years. All because I tried the "press and lift" test (shown below) and learned the secret of healthful Spirella support.

Press down on stomach. That's the cramped feeling of ordinary garments.

Now lower your hands and lift up! That's like Spirella's all day comfort.

How do you get this new comfort? Only from the Spirella Corsetiere who calls at your home. In quiet and privacy, while you're comfortably supported in a special modeling garment, she measures you for your Spirella.

For name of your local Spirella Corsetiere, write

In the U. S.
THE SPIRELLA CO., INC.
NIAGARA FALLS, N.Y.

In Canada
THE SPIRELLA CO., LTD.
NIAGARA FALLS, ONT.

303

Get a natural lift with Spirella

Claiming to "press and lift" the middle, 1949's Spirella girdles were said to make women "feel younger."

beauty under control

the Waistlette

So easy to whittle away your waist! An adjustable elastic band tops a gleaming satin panel to make you inches smaller. With exclusive Kant Roll keeping the top up, without boning—comfortably! In nude, black, white, blue. Small, Med., Large, Extra Large. Only $3.95 at fine stores

True Form
358 Fifth Ave., New York

Guaranteed by Good Housekeeping

In 1949, True Form advertised this waist-whittling corset without boning.

*SPORTIME GIRDLE. Natural rubber. Wear it under bathing suits, shorts, slacks or play clothes. Pantie style with perforated crotch. Petal Pink, Powder Blue, Gardenia White. Small, medium, large. $1.50.

A sports girdle designed by Kleinert's for wear under bathing suits or any other sports clothes. Made of rubber, it came in pink, blue, and white and was featured in the June 1949 issue of *Ladies' Home Journal.*

Real-form
GIRDLES OF GRACE

SKY-HI

if you're
5' 5"
or over

Designed
especially
for you tall gals.
Higher at the
waist, longer at the bottom . . .
with Thi-Kontrol, a special thigh
trimming and slimming feature
exclusive with Real-form. Raschel
knitted with nylon, rayon and Lastex.*
In pink and white, girdle and panty girdle,
sizes 26 to 32.
Front and back panels for firm control $6
Front panel for gentle control $5
Also with removable crotch.
If not available at your local store, write

REAL-FORM GIRDLE CO., Dept. U-1, 358 Fifth Avenue, New York 1

This Real-form ad from 1949 indicated girdles with front and back panels "for firm control" were available, as were "lighter" versions "for gentle control."

Slim, narrow Fall Fashions by America's greatest designers call for

NEW INVISIBLE PLAYTEX® LIVING® GIRDLE

INVISIBLE UNDER THE SLEEKEST CLOTHES, PLAYTEX COMBINES FIGURE-SLIMMING POWER WITH COMPLETE COMFORT.

New fashion silhouette is the slimmest in years. No longer are designers camouflaging little bulges at hip and thigh. Today, fashion *starts* with a woman's figure.

No other girdle slims and trims like PLAYTEX—with such comfort, such freedom of action. Made of tree-grown latex, PLAYTEX hasn't a single seam, stitch or bone. It's invisible under the sleekest fabrics, the slenderest skirts.

PLAYTEX washes in ten seconds, pats dry with a towel. And women say — if you wear PLAYTEX faithfully, the next PLAYTEX you buy will probably be a size smaller.

In slim, silvery tubes, PLAYTEX LIVING GIR-
DLES and PANTY GIRDLES with garters. Blossom Pink, Gardenia White, Heavenly Blue. Extra small, small, medium and large **$3.95**
PLAYTEX PANTY GIRDLE . . . **$3.50**
Extra Large PLAYTEX
 GARTER GIRDLE **$4.95**
Sensational PINK-ICE for extra coolness **$4.95**
*At all modern corset and notion
departments and better specialty shops*

INTERNATIONAL LATEX CORP'N.
Playtex Park, Dover, Del. ©1949

"The new fashion silhouette is the slimmest in years. No longer are designers camouflaging little bulges at hip and thigh," said a 1949 Playtex girdle ad. These girdles were made from "tree-grown latex" without seams or bones, and the ad claimed they washed "in ten seconds" and could be pat dried with a towel.

BEAU-BRA
NEW WAIST NIPPER

New Beau-Bra girdle combines the two most important features of the year. "CRISS-CROSS" for abdominal control and "WAIST NIPPER" for the new slender silhouette. Girdle #947. (Pantie #747) Small 23-25, Medium 26-28, Large 29-31 White, Tearose, Blue.
PRICE $2.99
Bra #276—Famous SKINNER'S SATIN— White, Blue, Pink, Orchid, Nile, Maize. A cup 32-36, B cup 32-38, C cup 34-40.
PRICE $1.69

The Beau-Bra was said to combine "the two most important features of the year. 'CRISS-CROSS' for abdominal control and 'WAIST NIPPER' for the new slender silhouette." As seen in the September 1949 issue of *Glamour*.

SLIMSTERS!
You're sleek 'n' free in "Skippies 3"

1. BRA 2. GIRDLE 3. PANTY. Feather-light and action-right... *exactly* as you want 'em... with a whisper of control and a world of comfort... *without* heavy bones! "Skippies 3" are downy-soft, tubbable, quick-drying. Panties and girdles come in a variety of elastic fabrics and lengths, with lots of styles and colors to choose from. Get a set to suit *you* today at any of the better stores.

1. Bras . . . . . *from* $1.75
2. Girdles . . . . *from* $3.00
3. Panties . . . . *from* $3.50
   (4 detachable garters)

P.S. If your mother's a slimster, remind her *she* can wear "Skippies 3," too!

THE FORMFIT COMPANY, CHICAGO, NEW YORK

"skippies 3" BY *Formfit*

The Formfit girdles of 1949 were designed for light support and lots of comfort—and the manufacturer stressed they were made "*without* heavy bones!"

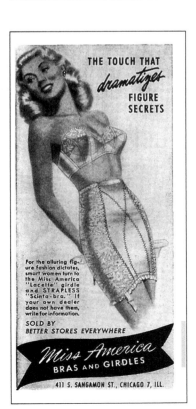

THE TOUCH THAT *dramatizes* FIGURE SECRETS

For the alluring figure fashion dictates, smart women turn to the Miss America "Lacette" girdle and STRAPLESS "Scinta-bra." If your own dealer does not have them, write for information.

SOLD BY BETTER STORES EVERYWHERE

Miss America BRAS AND GIRDLES
411 S. SANGAMON ST., CHICAGO 7, ILL.

A classic girdle of 1949, sold by Miss America Bras and Girdles.

Fashion Says: *"Look* Slim-Waisted!"

The new slim-waisted silhouette can be yours—beautifully, comfortably,
thanks to Sears corsetry! What does your figure need... modern, laced-in
corsets, or clever designs that shape you perfectly without lacings?
Choose from this gala array of grand values; Sears is the place to buy Corsets.

Ⓐ Laces a la 1940

$7.50
Value **$3.74**

Yes, you can whittle 2 or 3 inches from your waist in comfort! One of America's leading corset stylists designed this clever All-in-One, using only the softest and lightest of modern fabrics for control. Shimmering rayon and cotton satin front panel; matching back and side sections of light Darleen super-elastic. Net-lined bust, topped with filmy cotton lace. Flexible coiled wire boning. 4 long garters; front ones flat Invis-a-grip. Adjustable lacings, upper back; center front Talon closing. Front length, 19 in.; center back, 14 in. Wash in Lux. Nude color. Grand to dance in!

For Medium to Short Figures
Fits Hips 1 to 5 Inches
Larger Than Bust
Bust Sizes: 32, 33, 34, 35, 36, 37, 38 in. *State bust and hip measure.*
18 E 430—Shpg. wt., 12 oz. **$3.74**

Ⓑ Gorgeous Fit

$10.00
Value **$4.84**

Give yourself the new Victorian silhouette... high bust, curved-in waist, and long, sleek control over the hips! Exquisite materials and designing: lustrous rayon and cotton satin with inserts of matching Darleen super-elastic. The up-and-down stretch back and cross-stretch sides combine to mold your figure to new beauty. Lovely net-lined cotton lace bust. Talon-zip closing to waist; hooks from waist up. Tiny, adjustable front-lacings. Front garters have flat Invis-a-grip. Length over bust, 24½ in.; waist down, 15 in. Luxable. Newest Nude shade.

For Medium to Tall Figures—Fits
Hips 1 to 4 in. Larger Than Bust
Bust Sizes: 32, 33, 34, 35, 36, 37, 38, 39, 40, 41, 42 in. *State bust and hip measure; read Page 173.*
Shpg. wt., 1 pound 4 ounces.
18 E 450...................**$4.84**

**Read Madame La Mont's Letter and
"How To Measure" on Page 173
For Easy Terms, See Page 1038**

Ⓐ
The New "Wasp Waist" Corset with Clever Back-Lacings.

Ⓑ
The Glamorous "Hour Glass"
Cut Longer Over Hips

◉ SEARS PAGE 163

Waist whittling went in and out of fashion during the 1940s, along
with neo-Victorian dresses. In 1940, the *Sears, Roebuck and Co.* catalog
featured these girdles, both designed to trim the waist up to 3 inches.

Look like a new woman... stand beautifully erect
...take years off your figure, gracefully

Gale Health Belts

Gale Health Belts are approved by many doctors for wear after operations and childbirth . . . to help relieve that nagging backache . . . for general wear to give more lifting support than ordinary corsets.

And speaking of value, Mrs. Joseph J. Vacha of Quakertown, Pennsylvania writes: Your Gale Health Belt is the best for the least money, I've found. In shopping about, the $8.50 garments did not compare with it. I wear it every day in comfort.

How to Measure for Corsets
Please do not guess your size—use a tape measure. If you haven't a tape measure, Sears will send you one without charge. Measure waist at narrowest part over dress. Measure hips at fullest part over dress. State all measurements requested. See full Measuring Instructions on Page 173. For Maternity Corsets, see following page.

Famous *Gale* Two-Lace Model
Actual $6.50 Value **$2⁸⁴**

Scientifically designed for general wear, to help relieve backache and fatigue. Recommended for ptosis, umbilical hernia, after operations or childbirth. Fine pre-shrunk rayon brocaded coutil or cotton mesh. Non-rust boning. Cotton elastics top front. Two pull-strap cluster lacings. Side hooking. Tearose. Shpg. wt., 1 lb. 6 oz. *Reduced price.*
For Medium to Tall Figures—5 ft. 5 in. or more—
Fits Hips 7 to 10 Inches Larger Than Waist
Waist Sizes: 28, 29, 30, 31, 32, 33, 34, 35, 36, 37, 38, 39, 40, 41, and 42 in. *State waist and hip measure.* Front lgth., 11½ in.; back 15½ in.
18 E 595—*Rayon Brocaded Coutil*.........$2.84
18 E 295—*Strong Cotton Mesh*............ 2.84
For Short to Medium Figures—5 ft. 4 in. or less—
Fits Hips 7 to 10 Inches Larger Than Waist
Waist Sizes: 24, 25, 26, 27, 28, 29, 30, 31, 32, 33, 34, 35, 36 in. *State waist and hip; read Page 173.*
Front lgth., 10½ in.; back lgth., 15 in.
18 E 594—*Rayon Brocaded Coutil*.........$2.84
18 E 294—*Strong Cotton Mesh*............ 2.84

Also in Mesh

Gale Side Lace Thigh Control
$2⁹⁸
$5.00 Value
Three cluster-lacings for firm support to abdominal muscles. Well-boned; non-rust boning. Sturdy coutil. Tearose.
Fits Hips 8 to 12 Inches Larger Than Waist
Waist Sizes: 26, 27, 28, 29, 30, 31, 32, 33, 34, 35, 36, 37, 38; also 40 and 42 in. *State waist, hip measure.* Shpg. wt., 1 lb. 8 oz.
18 E 405—For Medium to Tall Figures—5 feet 5 inches or more. Length front, 11 in.; 16 in...................$2.98
18 E 215—For Short to Medium Figures—5 feet 4 inches or less. Length front, 10 in.; back, 15 in.................$2.98

Gale Girdle Type For Fuller Hips
$3⁷⁹
Hook Closing
$6.50 Value
Boned for abdominal support. Pre-shrunk rayon striped coutil. Two pull-strap back cluster lacings. Well-boned back. Cotton elastics. Overall length, 16½ in.; 2 in. above waist, 14½ in. waist down. Tearose.
Fits Hips 9 to 13 Inches Larger Than Waist
Waist Sizes: 27, 28, 29, 30, 31, 32, 33, 34, 35, 36, 37, 38, 39, 40 in. *State waist and hip measurements;* read How to Measure on Page 173. Shpg. wt., ea., 1 lb. 8 oz.
18 E 186—Convenient Talon closing. Step-in model.......$3.98
18 E 196—Side hook and eye closing. Wrap-around model..$3.79

Talon or Hook Closing

Gale Belt Lightweight
$2⁵⁹
$5.00 Value
Lightly boned support. Pre-shrunk rayon brocaded cotton batiste. Cotton and rayon elastic, top front. Side cluster lacings. Side hooking. Tearose. You'll like it!
Fits Hips 6 to 10 Inches Larger Than Waist
Waist Sizes: 24, 25, 26, 27, 28, 29, 30, 31, 32, 33, 34, 35, 36 in. *State waist and hip measure.* Shipping weight, each, 1 pound.
For Short to Medium Figures
Lgth. front, 9 in.; back, 13½ in.
18 E 246..................$2.59
For Medium to Tall Figures
Lgth. front, 10 in.; back, 15 in.
18 E 247..................$2.59

Gale Side-Lace Groin-Line Model
$3⁹⁸
$8.00 Value
Splendid abdominal support! 3 pull-strap lacings each side for better adjustment; smooth back. Helps relieve backache and muscle strain. Well-boned, non-rust boning. Pre-shrunk rayon brocaded coutil. Side hooking. Front length, 11½ in.; back, 17 in. Tearose.
For Medium to Tall Figures
Fits Hips 7 to 10 Inches Larger Than Waist
Waist Sizes: 32, 33, 34, 35, 36, 37, 38, 39, 40, 41, 42; also 44, 46, and 48 in. *State waist and hip measure;* read How to Measure on Page 173. Shpg. wt., 1 lb. 10 oz.
18 E 281..............$3.98

Gale Bra Back Lacing
$1²⁵
Lightly boned front for diaphragm control. Cluster lacings let you regulate uplift for comfort and proper support. Mercerized cotton batiste; built-up top. Wear with Gale belt or any waistline corset. Length center front, 11 in. Tearose.
For Full Bust Figure
Bust Sizes: 34, 36, 38, 40, 42, 44, 46 and 48 inches. *State size;* read How to Measure, Page 179. Shpg. wt., 9 oz.
18 E 616..............$1.25

◆ SEARS PAGE ₃185

These complicated girdles look like ancient contraptions but were common in catalogs from the 1940s.

De Luxe *Charmode*

In 4-Figure Styles **$2.84** Each

Tall Narrow Hips   Tall Full Hips   Short Normal Hips   Short Narrow Hips

Superior fit! . . . comfort! Boned coutil and mercerized cotton elastic inner belt. Pre-shrunk brocaded rayon and cotton batiste; non-rust boning. Tearose.
Bust Sizes: 34, 35, 36, 37, 38, 39, 40, 41, 42; also 44, 46, 48, 50, 52 and 54 inches. *State bust and hip measure; see* Page 173. Shpg. wt., ea., 1 lb. 11 oz.

Fits Normal Hips
3 to 6 Inches Larger Than Bust
18 E 567—Medium to Tall. Lgth. under arm, 20 in.; waist down, 15 in. . . $2.84
18 E 566—Short Figures. Lgth. under arm, 18 in.; waist down, 13 in. . . $2.84

Fits Narrow Hips
1 to 2 Inches Larger Than Bust
18 E 165—Short to Medium. Lgth. under arm, 19 in.; waist down, 14 in. $2.84

Fits Full Hips
5 to 7 Inches Larger Than Bust
18 E 587—*Tall Figures.* Length under arm, 21 in.; waist down, 16 in. . . $2.84

COILED WIRE Comfort Boning
Bends With Every Move

No Extra Charge for Laced Back

Boning Guaranteed Against Breakage for 6 Months

$3.39 10½-in. boned, side hooking inner belt, side lacings. Cotton and rayon elastics. Rayon brocaded coutil outer part. Coiled-wire boning. Laced back. Built-up top. Lgth. under arm 20-in.; waist down, 14½ in. Tearose.
For Medium to Tall Figures—Fits Hips 3 to 7 Inches Larger Than Bust
Bust Sizes: 35, 36, 37, 38, 39, 40, 41, 42 in.; also 44, 46, 48, and 50 in. *State bust and hip measure.* Shpg. wt., 1 lb. 13 oz.
18 E 409 . . . . $3.39

$1.98 Clasp front, boned inner belt, diagonal cotton elastics. Rayon-figured cotton cloth. Outer part has cotton and rayon side elastic sections. Coiled-wire boning. Length over bust, 23 in.; waist down, 14 in. Tearose.
For Medium to Tall Figures
Bust Sizes: 34, 35, 36, 37, 38, 39, 40, 41, 42; also 44, 46, 48 inches. *State bust, hip.*
Closed Back. Fits Hips 2 to 6 Inches Larger Than Bust
18 E 296—Shpg. wt., 1 lb. 6 oz. $1.98
Laced Back. Fits Hips 3 to 7 Inches Larger Than Bust
18 E 298—Shpg. wt., 1 lb. 6 oz. $1.98

SEARS PAGE 170

Sears Inner Belts

You will look so much younger and slimmer in a Sears Inner Belt Foundation!
Perfect control with all-day-long comfort

LUX P. S. We recommend gentle Lux to keep corsets dainty and better fitting

A Bargain . . . Cloth or Jersey Bust
$1.39 Each

Even at Sears, this is an exceptionally low price for a foundation of this quality. The cleverly designed 11½-inch inner belt with its diagonal-pull cotton elastic bands gives double control over waist and abdomen.
Rayon-figured cotton material outer garment, cotton elastic side panels, full length back boning. Length over bust to garter, 22 inches; waist down, 14 in. Tearose.
For Medium Figures—Fits Hips 2 to 5 Inches Larger Than Bust
Bust Sizes: 34, 36, 38, 40, 42, 44, 46, 48 in. *State bust and hip measures; read How to Measure on Page 173.* Shipping weight, each, 1 lb.
18 E 153—*Self-cloth Bust.* (large view) $1.39
18 E 155—*Rayon and Cotton Jersey bust* (small view) $1.39

Charmode Abdo-Control
Gives Wonderful Abdominal Support, Lacings Adjust for Perfect Fit
$2.98

Our popular Abdo-Control foundation, famous for supporting the back and abdomen in complete comfort! Diagonally-boned inner belt of strong coutil and mercerized cotton elastic, hooks at side. Outer garment of strong rayon-figured cotton coutil, reinforced in front, well-boned back. Back cluster lacings have pull straps for easy adjustment. Built-up top for better bust support, cotton elastic gore at top back for snug fit. $5.00 value. Tearose.
Fits Hips 5 to 7 In. Larger Than Bust
Bust Sizes: 36, 37, 38, 39, 40; also 42, 44, 46, 48, 50 in. *State bust and hip measure.* Shpg. wt., each, 2 lbs.
18 E 166—*Med. to Tall Figures.* Lgth. under arm, 20½ in.; waist down, 15 in. $2.98
18 E 163—*For Short Figures.* Lgth. under arm, 18½ in.; waist down, 13 in. $2.98

Girdles of this period were designed to flatten the stomach, smooth bulges—especially at the hips—and make the waist more trim. These girdles were featured in a 1940 *Sears, Roebuck and Co.* catalog.

Figure Control!

Makes Waist Smaller

Flattens Abdomen Diaphragm

Smooths Hip Bulges

Thrift Special
89c

We think this is the best foundation you'll find anywhere at this low price!

The 9½-in. inner-belt controls abdomen and diaphragm. Cotton elastic side panels in outer garment smooth hips and thighs. Full length back-boning.

Choice of cloth or cool cotton mesh, both safe in gentle *Lux.* Length over bust, 21½ in.; waist down, 13½ inches. Tearose.

For Short to Medium Figures
—Fits Hips 2 to 5 In.
Larger Than Bust

Bust sizes: 32, 34, 36, 38, 40, 42, 44 and 46 in. *State bust and hip measure;* Shpg. wt., ea., 13 oz.

18 E 359—Rayon Figured Cotton Fabric........89c
18 E 507—Cool Cotton Mesh Fabric..........89c

Also in Cool Mesh

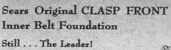

Sears Original CLASP FRONT Inner Belt Foundation

Still . . . The Leader!
Still . . . Unequaled!

Closed or Laced Back **$1.88** Each

Built-Up Bust

Made to Sears own specifications for quality! Molds you perfectly from bust to thigh. Well-made 12½-inch clasp front innerbelt has wide diagonal cotton elastic bands to control abdomen and diaphragm. Outer garment has special cloth reinforced front for extra diaphragm control. Well-boned back. Choice of fine rayon figured cotton fabric or cool cotton mesh. $3.00 value. Length over bust, 23 in.; waist down, 14½ in. Tearose. Wash in mild *Lux* suds for best results.

For Medium to Tall Figures
Bust Sizes: 34, 35, 36, 37, 38, 39, 40, 41, 42; also 44, 46, 48 in. *State bust and hip measure;* see How to Measure on Page 173. Shipping weight, each, 1 lb. 11 oz.

Closed Back—Fits Hips 2 to 5 Inches Larger Than Bust
18 E 302—Rayon Figured Cotton...$1.88
18 E 330—Cool Cotton Mesh....... 1.88

Laced Back—Fits Hips 3 to 7 Inches Larger Than Bust
18 E 306—Rayon Figured Cotton...$1.88
18 E 331—Cool Cotton Mesh....... 1.88

Built Up Bust
(small view above)
Closed Back—Fits Hips 2 to 5 Inches Larger Than Bust
18 E 305—Rayon Figured Cotton...$1.88

Everything Available on Sears Easy Payment Plan. See Page 1038.

For Shorter Figures 5 Ft. 3 In. or Less

Streamline Beauty for Shorter Women

$1.83 Each — Perfect control and comfort for the shorter woman! Rayon figured Luxable cotton fabric. Boned 9½-in. belt; boned back. Strong cotton elastic sides. Length over bust, 20½ in.; waist down, 12 in. Tearose.
Bust Sizes: 34, 36, 38, 40, 42, 44, 46, 48 in. *State bust and hip measure;* read Page 173. Shpg. wt., 14 oz.
Fits Hips 2 to 5 Inches Larger Than Bust
18 E 560—Closed Back.....$1.83
Fits Hips 3 to 6 inches Larger Than Bust
18 E 570—Laced Back.....$1.83

$2.79 — Pre-shrunk brocaded rayon and cotton batiste. Non-run Grip-Knit rayon and cotton elastics. Lustrous rayon and cotton jersey bust. 9-inch boned inner-belt has wide diagonal cotton elastic bands; well-boned back. Length over bust, 19 in.; waist down, 11 in. Safe in *Lux.* Tearose.
Fits Hips 2 to 5 Inches Larger Than Bust
Bust Sizes: 34, 35, 36, 37, 38, 39, 40; also 42, 44, 46, 48 in. *State bust and hip measure.*
18E164—Shpg. wt., 1 lb. 6 oz. $2.79

Separating Talon

$3.59 — Beautifully styled for perfect control. Strong preshrunk brocaded rayon and cotton batiste with fine mercerized cotton elastics and well-boned back. So easy to get on—Fastens in front with separating talon zip to waist; hooks and eyes to top. Boned coutil and cotton elastic inner-belt hooks at side. Use *Lux.* Length, 23½ in.; waist down, 15 in. Tearose.
For Medium to Tall Figures.
Fits Hips 2 to 5 In. Larger Than Bust
Bust Sizes: 34, 35, 36, 37, 38, 39, 40; also 42, 44, 46, 48 in. *State bust and hip measure;* read How to Measure, Page 173.
18 E 158—Shpg. wt., 1 lb. 12 oz. . . $3.59

Compare $3.00 Quality

$1.98 Each — Pre-shrunk rayon and cotton batiste. Boned, reinforced inner-belt. Tearose.
Even Bust Sizes: 34 to 48 in. *State bust and hip measure.* Shpg. wt., 1 lb., 1 oz.
For Medium to Tall Figures—Length over bust, 23½ in.; waist down, 15 in.
18 E 174—Closed Back..........$1.98
18 E 175—Laced Back........... 1.98
For Short Figures—Length over bust, 21½ in.; waist down, 13 in.
18 E 172—Closed Back..........$1.98

✪ SEARS PAGE 171

2-Way Stretch Dura-Latex Elastic For Fuller Figures

Ⓐ Laced "Kampus Girl"

$1.98 It's here! The nationally advertised "Kampus Girl" step-in for fuller figures! The same patented, boned-front inner shield, the same young lines—but knit of stronger 2-way stretch rayon and cotton Dura-Latex elastic. Lacings slim waist. Sells nationally for $2.50. Length about 15 in. Nude color.

For All Figure Heights
Sizes to Fit All Waists: 26 to 38 in. State waist, hip measure; read Page 173.
18 E 459—Shpg. wt., 14 oz.....$1.98

Ⓑ Sleek Front Talon

$1.88 A grand figure-slimmer! Does wonders for the fuller figure! Smooths hips, back and front bulges. Fine-quality 2-way stretch Dura-Latex Rayon and cotton elastic. Invisible front boning in rayon and cotton satin overlay, controls diaphragm, abdomen. Center Talon—slips on easily. Flat garters. $3.00 quality. Length, 15 in. Tearose.

For All Figure Heights
Sizes to Fit All Waists: 28 to 40 in. State waist, hip measure; read Page 173.
18 E 578—Shpg. wt., 15 oz.....$1.88

Panty or Girdle

$1.19 Talon Bargains! Firm, comfy; good, 2-way stretch Dura-Latex cotton elastic. Boned front shield. Short bones at top back prevent top rolling. Lgth., 15 in. Tearose. *Sizes to Fit All Waists: 28 to 40 in. State waist, hip.* Shpg. wt., ea., 7 oz.

With Talon Zip Closing
(C)18 E 344—Panty; no garters..$1.19
(D)18 E 334—Girdle; 4 garters.. 1.19

Without Talon Zip Closing
(C)18 E 383—Panty; no garters...89c
(D)18 E 593—Girdle; 4 garters Ea...89c

Swish your girdles through gentle Lux suds and they'll come out lovely-looking. Lux helps preserve elasticity.

Buy several corsets now and be ready for Spring. $2 a month pays for any $10 to $17 order. For Easy Terms, see Page 1038.

Slim Your Waist

Detachable Crotch and Garters

Power Net
$2.84 Front and back of up-and-down stretch rayon and cotton Darleen super-elastic. Sides of 2-way stretch power net Lastex. Boned front shield. Talon. Lgth., 14 in. Tearose.

For Short to Medium Figures
Fits Hips 7 to 10 Inches Larger Than Waist
Waist Sizes: 24, 25, 26, 27, 28, 29, 30, 31, 32, 33, 34. *State waist and hip measure.* Shipping weight, each, 13 oz.
18 E 489.........$2.84
18 E 332—Similar to above, but with open stitch 2-way cotton elastic.......$1.98

Panty Girdle
$1.98 Soft rayon and cotton satin Darleen super-elastic. Sides and front stretch cross-wise; back stretches up-and-down, for better control. Lightly-boned front. Talon zip. Luxable. Length, 14½ inches. Tearose.

Fits Hips 6 to 10 Inches Larger Than Waist
All Waist Sizes: 25, 26, 27, 28, 29, 30, 31, 32, 33, 34 in. *State waist, hip.* Shpg. wt., 11 oz.
18 E 419.......$1.98
18 E 422—Extra crotch. Shpg. wt., 2 oz.....25c

Talon or Lace
$1.88 14-in. 2-way stretch, wo en cotto elastic girdle. Bone front. Use Lux. Tearos

Fits Hips 7 to 10 Inches Larger Than Waist
Waist Sizes: 26, 27, 2 29, 30, 31, 32, 33, 3 35, 36 in. *State waist, h* Shpg. wt., ea., 11 oz.

Short to Medium Figure 14-Inch Length
18 E 572—Talon..$1.8
18 E 361—Side lace. 1.8

Medium to Tall Figures 16-Inch Length
18 E 573—Talon...$2.1
18 E 364—Side lace. 2.1

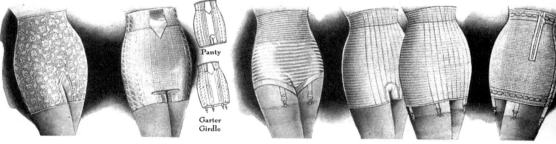

Panty

Garter Girdle

Lace Lastex Panty
$1.88 Light, boneless! Cotton lastex stretches to give pretty figure curves! Silk Milanese crotch. No garters. Length, 15 inches. Tearose.
Sizes to Fit All Waists: from 23 to 32 inches. Be sure to state waist and hip measure when ordering. Read Page 173. Shipping weight, 9 ounces.
18 E 492 ....$1.88

Bargains—3 Styles
49c Ea. Such grand values, you will want to buy all three styles. Soft knit, 2-way stretch Dura-Latex cotton elastic. Reinforced in front with rayon and cotton satin. Splendid for sports and everyday wear. Luxable. Length, 15 in. Tearose. *Sizes to Fit All Waists: 23 to 34 in. State waist and hip measure.* Shpg. wt., 7 oz.
18E523—Leg-Band Panty. No garters.49c
18E529—Crotch Panty. No garters...49c
18E528—Girdle with 4 garters.......49c

"Tummy-In" Panty
69c Light, boneless! Run-resistant, rayon satiny-striped jersey. 6-inch top of 2-way stretch cotton elastic to hold tummy in. Soft, double crotch; detachable garters. Use Lux. Length, 14 in. Tearose. *Sizes to Fit All Waists: 23 to 34 in. State waist and hip measure.* Shipping weight, 7 ounces.
18 E 141...............69c

Thrift Specials
35c Ea. Buy both girdle and panty! Marvelously comfortable; no bones, no seams. The 2-way stretch cotton elastic is far better quality than usual at this price. Length, 15 in. Tearose. *Sizes to Fit All Waists: 23 to 30 in. State waist, hip measure.* Shipping weight, each, 5 oz.
18 E 328—Garter Girdle. .35c
18 E 329—Panty; no garters35c

In 3 Lengths
88c 12-in. Firm cotton tic girdles, ple of stretch. T zip. No bones. Tearose. *Fits Hips 8 to 12 Inches Larger Than Waist*
All Waist Sizes: 24 to 30 32, 34 in. *State waist, hip;* Page 173. Shpg. wt., ea., 1
18 E 493—12-inch.......
18 E 494—14-inch.......
18 E 495—16-inch.....$

SEARS PAGE **176**

Lightweight girdles from a 1940 *Sears, Roebuck and Co.* catalog. Also note the waist cinchers. The "Tiny Waisted" is really a short Victorian corset.

Wear a Sears Girdle!

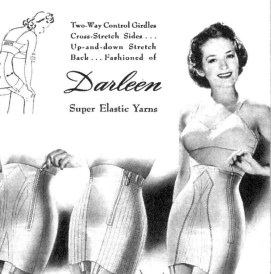

Two-Way Control Girdles
Cross-Stretch Sides...
Up-and-down Stretch
Back...Fashioned of

Darleen
Super Elastic Yarns

Three Lengths

Fashion's Newest! Higher-Waisted Laced-in Girdles

Tearose or White

Laces in Front

$2.84 ea. (A) Built up 2 inches above the waist, 15 in. below. Lightly boned front and clever lacing to nip-in your waist. Rayon and cotton satin with matching batiste Darleen super-elastic sides. For Medium to Tall—Fits Hips 7 to 11 In. Larger Than Waist *Waist Sizes:* 25, 26, 27, 28, 29, 30, 31, 32, 33, 34, 35 and 36 in. *State waist and hip measure.* Shpg. wt., 1 lb.
18 E 428—Tearose ...$2.84
18 E 429—White 2.84

Tiny-Waisted

$1.25 (B) Short Victorian girdle. Lightly-boned rayon and cotton batiste with matching Darleen super-elastic sides. Side hook; back lace. Front length about 10 in. *Waist Sizes:* 24, 26, 28, 30, 32 in. *State waist measure.* Shpg. wt., 6 oz.
18 E 503—Nude color. $1.25

Laced in Back

$2.98 (C) "Empire Fashion" girdle cut 2 in. above waist, 15 in. below waist with short back lacings to slim your waist. Pre-shrunk rayon and cotton batiste, decorated front with matching Darleen super-elastic sides, boned front and back. For Medium to Tall—Fits Hips 7 to 11 In. Larger Than Waist *All Waist Sizes:* 26, 27, 28, 29, 30, 31, 32, 33, 34, 35 and 36 in. *State waist and hip measure.* Shpg. wt., 1 lb. 2 oz.
18 E 498—Nude color. $2.98

Value Leader

$1.88 Cleverly designed hip-slimming girdle. Rayon and cotton Darleen super-elastic, cross-stretch sides, up-and-down stretch back. Boned rayon and cotton satin front panel. Easy action. Talon zip closing. Wash in Lux. Length, 15 inches. Tearose. For Medium to Tall Figures Fits Hips 7 to 10 Inches Larger Than Waist *Waist Sizes:* 25, 26, 27, 28, 29, 30, 31, 32, 33, 34 in. *State waist and hip measure.* Read "How to Measure," Page 173. Shpg. wt., 10 oz.
18 E 588.........$1.88

Non-Roll Top

$2.84 Tiny bones at top prevent rolling. Front and back of Rayon and Cotton Satin, up-and-down stretch, Darleen super-elastic; sides of open weave, 2-way stretch cotton elastic. Boned-front shield flattens tummy. Side Talon. Length, 15 in. Tearose. For Medium to Tall Fits Hips 6 to 10 Inches Larger Than Waist *Waist Sizes:* 25, 26, 27, 28, 29, 30; also 32, 34 in. *State waist and hip measure.* Shpg. wt., 12 oz.
18 E 453.......$2.84

Usually $5.00

$2.84 14-in. Sleek-fitting girdle of finer quality Darleen super-elastic sides and back. Matching cloth front is beautifully stitched and lightly boned. Talon zip closing. Nude color. Fits Hips 7 to 11 In. Larger Than Waist *Waist Sizes:* 26, 27, 28, 29, 30, 31, 32, 33, 34, 35, 36 in. *State waist, hip.* Shpg. wt., 1 lb. 2 oz.
Rayon and Cotton Satin
18 E 546—14 in .. $2.84
18 E 547—16 in .. 3.39
Rayon and Cotton Batiste
18 E 125—15 in.. $2.98

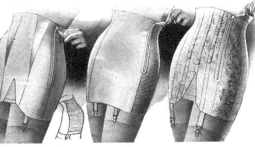

2-way Back

98c Lightly-boned cotton batiste front; 2-way cotton elastic back. Length. 14 in. Shpg. wt., 9 oz. Tearose. Short to Medium Figures Fits Hips 7 to 10 Inches Larger Than Waist *All even and odd Waist Sizes:* 26 to 34 in. *State waist, and hip.*
18 E 370...........98c

2 Lengths

94c 12-in. Celanese Rayon Satin. sateen lined. Open weave cotton elastic; lightly boned front. Tearose. Talon zip. Fits Hips 7 to 10 Inches Larger Than Waist *All Waist Sizes:* 25 to 34 in. *State waist and hip.* Shpg. wt., ea. 8 oz.
18 E 391—12 in..... 94c
18 E 392—13½ in. $1.00

Rare Bargain

98c Boned brocaded rayon and cotton batiste. Knitted cotton and rayon elastic sides. Lgth. 14 in. Tearose. For Medium Figures—Fits Hips 7 to 11 Inches Larger Than Waist *Even and odd Waist Sizes:* 26 to 36 in. *State waist, hip.* Shpg. wt., 12 oz.
18 E 317...........98c

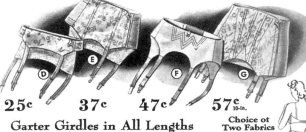

25c (D) **37c** (E) **47c** (F) **57c** (G) 10-in.

Choice of Two Fabrics

Garter Girdles in All Lengths

(D) Holds your stockings up neatly and trimly! Brocaded rayon and cotton batiste. Two-inch cotton elastic sides. Boneless. Four long garters. Side hook. Wash in Lux. It pays to buy two and change often. Tearose. *Even Waist Sizes:* 24, 26, 28, 30, 32, 34 in. *State waist size;* read How to Measure on Page 173. Shipping weight, each, 4 ounces.
18 E 338—Each......25c   2 for..47c

(E) Brocaded rayon and cotton batiste. 6-inch cotton elastic sides. Light, front boning; boneless back 9¼ in. Four strong garters. Side hook. Lux care will keep garter-belts dainty, better fitting. Tearose. *Waist Sizes:* 24, 25, 26, 27, 28, 29, 30; also 32, 34 in. *State waist measure.* Read "How to Measure," Page 173. Shpg. wt., ea., 7 oz.
18 E 378—Each......37c   2 for...70c

(F) Pre-shrunk rayon and cotton batiste. 2-in. cotton elastic at back; hooks at back. Lgth. 5 in. Tearose. Shpg. wt., ea., 4 oz. *Waist Sizes:* 24, 26, 28, 30, 32 in. *State size.*
18 E 318—Each.........47c   2 for...90c

(G) Lightly-boned front, cotton elastic sides. Boneless back. Tearose. *All Waist Sizes:* 24 to 30 in.; also 32, 34 in. *State waist and hip.* Shpg. wt., ea., 7 oz.

Brocaded Rayon and Cotton Batiste
18 E 311—10 in. Each.57c   2 for...$1.10
18 E 411—12 in. Each.69c   2 for... 1.30

Lustrous Rayon and Cotton Satin
18 E 386—10 in. Each.57c   2 for...$1.10
18 E 387—12 in. Each.69c   2 for... 1.30

(★) SEARS PAGE 177

1940 Fashion Says...

Laces whittle inches off your waist . . .

Keep corsets fresh and dainty with LUX
Why not buy that extra corset on Sears Easy Terms

Our Finest C.H.&S.

Comfort — Health — Style

Back Lacer

- Extra Strong Coutil
- Well Reinforced Front
- Firm, Flexible Boning

$1.78

A triumph in value-giving! Remarkable quality at Sears low price. Gives splendid abdominal control; slims waist and rounds hips beautifully.

Firm, flexible boning; extra-strong coutil. Reinforced front; thigh control straps. Cotton and rayon elastics. Front clasp. 6 garters. Tearose.

Fits Hips 9 to 13 In. Larger Than Waist *Waist Sizes:* 25, 26, 27, 28, 29, 30, 31, 32; also 34, 36, 38, 40, 42 in. *State waist and hip measure,* read How to Order below. Shipping wt., each. 1 lb. 10 oz.

Med. to Tall Figures Front length, 13 in.; side and back, 16¾ in. 18 E 235......$1.78

For Short Figures Front length, 11 in.; side and back length, about 14½ inches. 18 E 234......$1.78

Two Lengths for All Heights

How to Order Back and Front Lace Corsets
Don't allow for spread of laces; state actual waist and hip measurements taken snugly over dress. Use a tape measure. If you haven't one, Sears will send you one without charge. For additional Measuring Instructions, see Page 173.

Front Zip Closing

Fine Figure Controlling C.H.&S. Lace Corsets

New "Little-Waist" Back Lace Girdle

$1.79

(A) Made 4 to 5 in. above the waist; it raises the bust, slims waist, and rounds hips. Plush-faced Talon fastener; step-in model. Pre-shrunk rayon brocaded cotton batiste; rayon satin trimmed top. Light, non-rust boning. Front lgth., 14 in.; laced back, 11½ in. Flat garters; 2 in front, 2 in back. Tearose.

For All Height Figures *Waist Sizes:* 24, 25, 26, 27, 28 29, 30, 31, 32 in. *State waist and hip measures.* Shpg. wt., 1 lb. 18 E 260...............$1.79

New, Modern Talon-Front Corset

$1.98

(B) New high-waisted back lacer! Gives your figure the newest lines. Smooth Talon front, comfortable lightweight non-rust boning. Fine cotton batiste, rayon satin top trim. Cotton and rayon elastic gores bottom front. 4 flat garters. $3.00 value. Made 2½ in. above waist at front, 3 in. at back; overall length, front, 15 in.; back, 17 in. New Nude color.

Medium to Tall.. Fits Hips 8 to 12 in. Larger Than Waist *Waist Sizes:* 25, 26, 27, 28, 29, 30, 31, 32, 33, 34, 35 and 36 inches. *State waist and hip measure,* read How to Order at left. Shipping weight, 1 lb. 2 oz. 18 E 218...............$1.98

C.H.&S.

Comfort — Health — Style

Pull-Strap Control Back Lace Model

$1.98

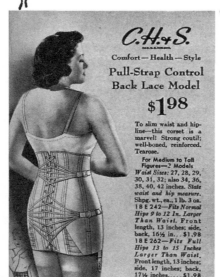

To slim waist and hip-line—this corset is a marvel! Strong coutil; well-boned, reinforced. Tearose.

For Medium to Tall Figures—2 Models *Waist Sizes:* 27, 28, 29, 30, 31, 32; also 34, 36, 38, 40, 42 inches. *State waist and hip measure.* Shpg. wt., ea., 1 lb. 3 oz.

18 E 242—*Fits Normal Hips 9 to 12 In. Larger Than Waist.* Front length, 13 inches; side, back, 16½ in... $1.98

18 E 262—*Fits Full Hips 13 to 15 inches Larger than Waist.* Front length, 13 inches; side, 17 inches; back, 17½ inches.....$1.98

SEARS PAGE 182

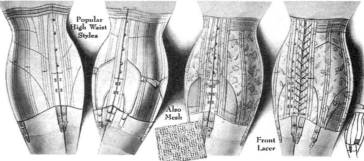

Popular High Waist Styles

Also Mesh

Front Lacer

Special Value	Thigh Control	$1.29 Value	Smooth Back
94c	**$1.59**	**94c** Ea.	**$1.88**
Sturdy cotton twill. Reinforced; well-boned. Front clasp,.9 in.; medium high bust, 3½ in.; overall front length, 14 in.; back length, 16½ in. Tearose color.	Adjustable thigh straps. Good quality coutil, well-boned. Back lacing. High bust, 4 in.; front lgth., 16¼ in.; back lgth., 17¾ in. Clasp, 11 in. Tearose.	Style and quality at a low price! Adjustable back laces. 13-in. front, 15 in. back. Tearose.	Pre-shrunk rayon brocaded cotton batiste. Cotton and rayon elastics. Front clasp, 7½ in. Front lgth., 14 in.; back, 17 in. Tearose.
Medium to Tall Figures— Fits Hips 9 to 13 In. Larger Than Waist *Waist Sizes:* 24, 25, 26, 27, 28, 29, 30, 31, 32, 33, 34, 35, 36, 37, 38, 39, 40 in. *State waist and hip measure.* 18E241-Shpg.wt.,14 oz.94c	Medium to Tall Figures Fits Hips 9 to 13 In. Larger Than Waist *Waist Sizes:* 25, 26, 27, 28,29, 30, 31, 32, 34, 36, 38, 40, 42 in. *State waist, hip.* Shpg.wt., 1 lb. 2 oz. 18 E 205.......$1.59	For Medium Figures .. Fits Hips 9 to 13 In. Larger Than Waist *Waist Sizes:* 25, 26, 27, 28, 29, 30, 31, 32; also 34, 36, 38 in. *State waist and hip.* Shpg. wt., ea., 12 oz. 18 E 214—Rayon Brocaded Cotton Batiste.....94c 18 E 216—Self Figured Cotton Mesh.........94c	For Medium to Tall— Fits Hips 9 to 13 In. Larger Than Waist *Waist Sizes:* 26, 27, 28, 29, 30, 31, 32, 33, 34, 35, 36, 37, 38 in. *State waist and hip measures.* Shpg. wt.. 1 lb. 1 oz. 18 E 240.......$1.88

A true corset with a zipper front is featured on this page from a 1940 Sears catalog, as well as stomach belts, and spiral steel boned girdles.

As advertised in a 1950 issue of *Good Housekeeping*, this Naturflex girdle sold for between $1 and $1.98.

This 1950 Bestform girdle was made from "flexible, airy nylon" and would give wearers "a waist worth buying a belt for."

LILY OF FRANCE

Cormiere

...TOO BEAUTIFUL   TO BE CALLED A CORSET

There's a change in the fashion world.
The corset has emerged from its chrysallis.
Cormiere is its name . . . beautiful creation with
elegant French touches. Ribbons and satins
and embroidery . . . Cormiere . . . to pleasingly
slim you. mold you in one smooth,
unbroken line. All-in-one of power net . . . 29.50.
Also available with shoulder straps.

ЅTRADEMARK

High top panty of sheer nylon elastic, 12.50
Bra . . . nylon taffeta, nylon lace trim, 3.00

Hi-Hi waisted of sheer nylon elastic, 18.50
Bra . . . satin and nylon lace, 5.00

Four-section of point d'esprit Power Bobbinette
and nylon voile, 18.50.   Bra . . . nylon voile, 3.50

Lily of France called these 1952 girdles "too beautiful to be called a corset."

to Smart Women
who Shop for Fashion...

this flexees girdle at $12.95
is today's first choice!

It's the *shape* that *makes* the *fashion* . . .
and makes all fashions *fit* better. It's
Flatterin'-Hi Girdle . . . created by
Flexees . . . of wisp-light nylon power
net—for greater beauty, *blissful ease.*
One glance and you'll see it's a *rare*
value: **$12.95.** Flexees wired,
deep-plunge strapless Bra . . .
glamour-shaper. Of embroidered
nylon and nylon marquisette: **$3.95**
Each a beauty . . . in white or black.
Ask your favorite store for Flexees!

flexees

Available in black or white, this 1952 girdle cost $12.95 and was made by Flexees.

The WITCHING POWER

A new Warner-Wonderful original in imported Chantilly lace and powernet.

Elegant as it is effective, this is Warner's freedom-loving translation

of the new linear look ... with a French accent.

See how world-famous Warner's coaxes your midriff into longer lines

with carefree comfort ... makes you *fit* for *fashion.*

WARNER'S*

Bras · Girdles · Corselettes

*REG. U. S. PAT. OFF.

Proving girdles could be beautiful as well as slimming was this 1952
Warner's creation, made from Chantilly lace and powernet.

• Under a bare dress,
a strapless brassiere that
reaches to the waist—
embroidered nylon
marquisette, cut very
low in front. $8.95.
The girdle, white nylon
strengthened both
front and back
with panels of rayon
satin. $10.95.
Both by Flexees, at Altman.

Harper's Bazaar described this 1952 girdle as being made of white nylon, "strengthened both front and back with panels of rayon satin. $10.95" by Flexees.

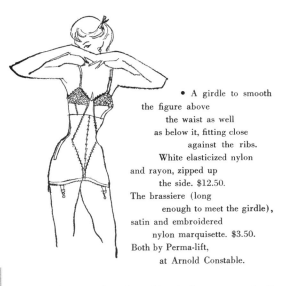

• A girdle to smooth
the figure above
the waist as well
as below it, fitting close
against the ribs.
White elasticized nylon
and rayon, zipped up
the side. $12.50.
The brassiere (long
enough to meet the girdle),
satin and embroidered
nylon marquisette. $3.50.
Both by Perma-lift,
at Arnold Constable.

Fitted close to the ribs, this girdle was made from white elasticized nylon and rayon, with a zipper. It sold for $12.50 from Perma-lift.

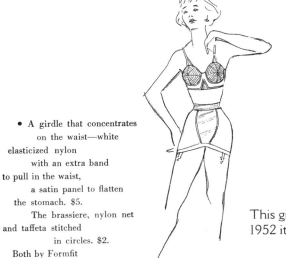

• A girdle that concentrates
on the waist—white
elasticized nylon
with an extra band
to pull in the waist,
a satin panel to flatten
the stomach. $5.
The brassiere, nylon net
and taffeta stitched
in circles. $2.
Both by Formfit
at May Company, Cleveland.

Girdles had a tendency to either roll down at the waist or ride up at the bottom. This 1955 Perma-lift girdle promised to do neither.

This girdle "concentrates on the waist," and in 1952 it sold for $5 from May Company.

The Girdle That Will Launch a Thousand Shapes

LOUISE DAHL-WOLFE

• Allover shaping is just about the most important fashion accessory now. Clothes with the new narrow lines ask for more than a cinch—the whole body must take on a longer line, a smoothness that starts above the waist and reaches way below it. THE HIGH-WAISTED GIRDLE (right) that controls inches north and south of the waist. Black nylon power net and embroidered marquisette. About $25. The brassiere, black nylon embroidered lightly with flowers. About $4. Both by Lily of France. THE HIGH-WAISTED GIRDLE (opposite) nylon elastic that brings the diameter of the waist down, and flattens generally by means of diamond insets (rayon and satin elastic). About $14. The lacy brassiere, black nylon over pink. About $5. Both by Lily of France. All four at Saks Fifth Avenue, New York; Julius Garfinckel; I. Magnin; Marshall Field; Sakowitz. For a list of stores in other cities, see page 255.

HARPER'S BAZAAR, OCTOBER 1952

"Allover shaping is just about the most important fashion accessory now," wrote the editors of *Harper's Bazaar* in October of 1952. This high-waisted girdle (right) was made of embroidered black power net and sold for about $25 from Lily of France.

"Not so long ago a corset was a monstrous thing made of whalebone, steel, and lacing," wrote the editors of *Today's Woman* in 1953. Naturally, they felt modern corsets emphasized "the natural look." This long-waisted girdle is paired with a bra with "elastic diaphragm control."

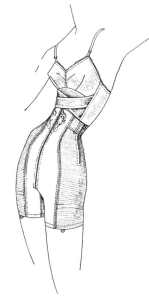

A long line bra that smoothly met the girdle, from the October 1952 issue of *Today's Woman*.

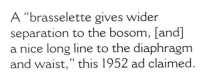

A "brasselette gives wider separation to the bosom, [and] a nice long line to the diaphragm and waist," this 1952 ad claimed.

A seamless, boneless latex girdle from 1953.

Skippies girdles, made by Formfit, were "penny-wise" at just $3.95 and up in 1953.

the new
American figure
from head to toe

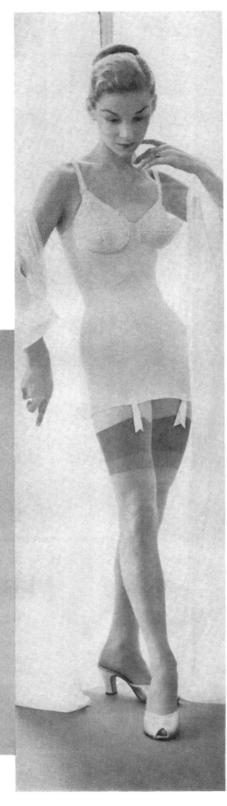

For the new slim look—this all-in-one corselet of featherweight elastic is designed to give comfortable control without bones or extra reinforcements

Stockings, Burlington
Slippers, Daniel Green
Robe, Schiaparelli

Sheer wool printed in Paisley design for fall. Collarless dress has elbow-length sleeves. Black on royal blue or red. 10-18, about $25. Jerry Gilden At Joseph Magnin, San Francisco

Hat, John Frederics
Gloves, Dawnelle
Bag, Astrid
Shoes, Delmanette
Stockings, Diamond

OCTOBER 1953

"The new American figure from head to toe," the editors of *Today's Woman* proclaimed in 1953, featuring an "all-in-one corselet of featherweight elastic to give comfortable control without bones or extra reinforcement."

FOR THE FIRST TIME IN 5,000 YEARS—

a girdle that slims
so much—
so comfortably...

and without bones!

PETER PAN

Egyptian Queen†

At last—the first *all* elastic, boneless girdle that brings you comfort as you like it *plus* control where you need it!

• An inch or more off your waistline and hipline! Take the tape-measure test—and see the difference!

• Exclusive elastic "muscles" with X-tra support at those important places where these elastic bands cross. (see diagram)

All styles...from 8.95 to 18.50

Her bra is Hidden Treasure*, of course!

PETER PAN FOUNDATIONS, INC. • NEW YORK 16

†TRADEMARK ⊕REG. U.S. PAT. OFF.

Elastic as a second skin—

Keeps derrière

and tummy in!

PETER PAN

Another great exclusive by the creators of Hidden Treasure*, Inner Circle*, and Merry-Go-Round* bras.

CHARM June, 1955

The Peter Pan girdle claimed to be the first girdle without any bones, made entirely of elastic. It also claimed to cinch in the waist by one inch. As advertised in the June 1955 issue of *Charm*.

Just picture yourself

in **3-D** wearing a *Lewella*

convertible sports bra...

...*with true bra construction*

...a lens eye view of you smartly attired for leisure ... for smart sportswear. In easy-to-care for Dan River WRINKL-SHED Poplin.

=325 — Padded, A and B cups. Red, Navy, White. $2.00

=320—As above without padding. $2.00

STRAPLESS BRA!

Lewella FITS YOU and YOUR BUDGET too!

CONVENTIONAL BRA!

CRISS-CROSS HALTER!

HALTER TOP BRA!

=321 — 4' band. B and C cups. Red, Navy, White. $2.00

=411 — Padded, A and B cups. Red or navy. $1.50

=400 — Halter style, contrasting white trim. A and B cups. Red or navy. $1.00

Send for your FREE copy of "Lewella's Secrets of Figure Loveliness." Write Dept. J-C.

LEWEL MFG. CO.
149 MADISON AVENUE, NEW YORK 16, N.Y.

Although this 1955 garment was considered a bra, it resembled a corset, complete with boning.

Made of breathable, pretty lace, this "braselette" sold for $5.95 in 1955.

Just as Victorian women wore corsets under their bathing suits, women in the 1950s often wore girdles. A 1955 *Charm* editorial claimed this girdle was "invisible under the sleekest suit, a latex panty girdle shaped to smooth the way for a closely figured swimsuit…It has a non-roll top, no bones or garters, is fabric-lined and perforated."

NYLON ALL-IN-ONE
bares your shoulders $10⁹⁸

Half bra with oval wires and lovely embroidered nylon sheer cups tops a slimming
all-in-one. Nylon Lastex side panels and
a walk-free front gore are embroidered
nylon sheer. Long zipper back closing
and SIX ribboned garters. White or black.

A Cup: 32-36 B Cup: 32-42 C Cup: 32-42

An all-in-one garment, combining bra and
girdle. Made of nylon, it cost $10.98 in 1955.

WHITTLES DOWN
YOUR WAISTLINE
INSTANTLY
INCHES
SEEM TO
DISAPPEAR

NEW!
French Figure
REDUCER

Its secret magic laces give you a fresh custom-made fitting every day. Adjustable to daily changes in your figure.
Superbly made of fine fabrics which absorb perspiration
and help keep you cool. French Figure REDUCER is guaranteed to keep its stretch and shape. Will not roll or
curl at the top. Washes like a dream.
Molds your figure into Fashion's Newest Silhouette;
inches seem to disappear from waist, hips $4.98
and thighs with the greatest of ease and comfort, sitting or stretching.
        IN NUDE, WHITE and BLUE
Reg. Girdle or Panty Girdle, snap-bottom crotch and garters.
Small (25-26), Med. (27-28), Large (29-30), Ex. Large
(31-32).
"Plus" sizes for the fuller figure: XX (33-35), XXX
(36-38), XXXX (39-40), XXXXX (41-43), XXXXXX
(44-46).

Hearkening back to laced up Victorian
corsets, this 1955 girdle was designed to
whittle the waist.

Supporting an American Princess on a Holiday:
Warner's very new Le Gant.° And what wonderful support—gentle and comfortable, yet persuasive and reas-
suring. High-waisted, with a stretch back, and a uniquely
designed front lace panel. Beguiling on its own, it's a
delicate combination of Brazilian Brown with ecru.
Nylon lace, marquisette and sheer power net. #921;
also in white . . . $25.00. Matching bra, #1021 . . . $7.50.

LINGERIE: VANITY FAIR

Girdle and bra by WARNER'S*
*REG. U.S. PAT. OFF.

"Beguiling on its own," this Warner's girdle was
fashioned from deep brown and ecru nylon lace
and cost $25. As featured in the November 1955
issue of *Harper's Bazaar*.

A long-line, strapless bra worn with a Lastex girdle, from 1955.

A 1955 *Harper's Bazaar* editorial on foundations noted that "to judge from this autumn's collections—or from a glance along any city street from noon to midnight—black is better, if possible, than ever." Among the many black girdles featured was this one piece wonder with power net and satin elastic.

Made from black Sacron elastic with boning, this 1955 lacy girdle cost about $15 from Bali.

Embroidered with rosebuds, this girdle was designed for slender women and cost about $8.95 from Gossard in 1955.

HI-NESS® by RITE-FORM

MEANS FASHION FOR SIZES 27 to 40

Designed for today's straight-lined fashions — Rite-Form's superb Hi-Ness shapes the fuller feminine figure into brilliant new proportions . . . and demonstrates a powerful inch-whittling strength in its Talon zipped embroidered nylon sheer front panel, extra-supporting thigh gussets, up-and-down stretch lastik back, leno nylon lastik sides. Sizes 27 to 40. In white or pink, about 15.00; in black, about 16.50. To complete the ensemble: the Hi-Ness brassiere of lace and fine nylon lastik — with deep five inch band. Sizes 34 to 48 in B, C, and D cups. Pink, white, or black. About 5.95. At fine stores, or write to Rite-Form, 64 West 23rd Street, New York 10, New York.

"Designed for today's straight-lined fashions" this Rite-Form whittled the waist, flattened the stomach, and controlled the thighs. It was available in white, pink, or black and sold for $15 to $16.50 in 1955.

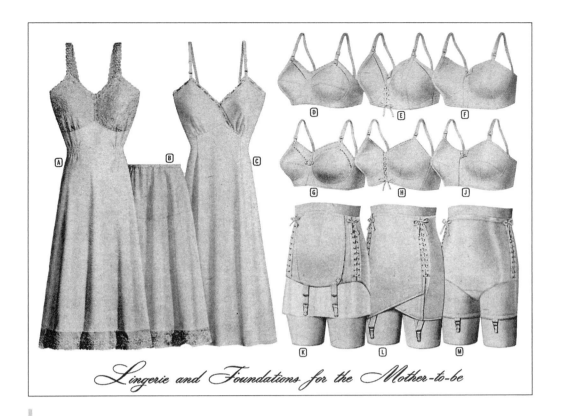

Lingerie and Foundations for the Mother-to-be

"Scientifically designed maternity supports" from the Fall & Winter 1956–57 *Montgomery Ward* catalog. The lacing along the sides, for a growing stomach, show maternity corsets hadn't changed much since the Victorian era.

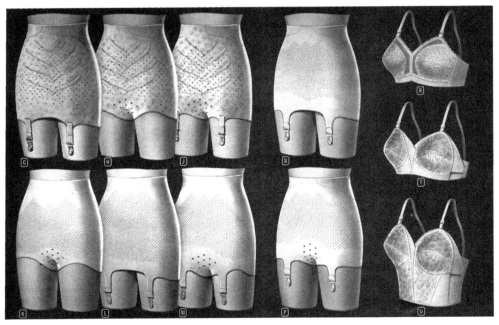

Playtex...Fits as if Made for You

Playtex girdles from a 1956 *Montgomery Ward* catalog. G through J were without seams or bones made of latex and cotton and costing $7.95 to $8.95. K through M were for light control, made of latex and cotton, and cost almost $5. N through P had non-roll tops and were made of latex and cotton, and cost $5.95 to $6.95.

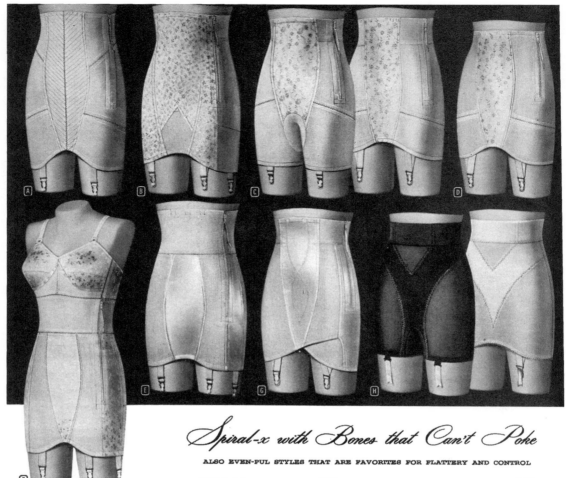

Spiral-x with Bones that Can't Poke

ALSO EVEN-PUL STYLES THAT ARE FAVORITES FOR FLATTERY AND CONTROL

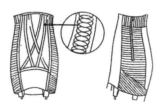

SPIRAL-X CONTROL

- Coils of flexible spiral wire eliminate poky bones.
- Tummy is smoothed, flattened in new comfort.
- Boning is sewn in natural curves (sketch at left).
- Controlling Spiral wire (see inset) will not poke.
- Bends with every move; amazing ease, freedom.
- Cross-stretch Leno elastic sides (sketch at right).
- Fagoted bias elastic at hipline will not ride up.
- Up-and-down-stretch back is contour-curved.
- Joan Browne Measuring Instructions on Pg. 226.

SPIRAL-X FASHIONABLE HIGH WAIST 8.95

(A) ELASTIC MIDRIFF-MOLDING. Cut high above waist to taper midriff, plus the new Spiral-X non-poke tummy control. Spiral-X flexible wire, skillfully sewn in curves, flattens abdomen smoothly; bends with every move for more comfort and control than you've ever known before. Front panel of stitched Nylon Taffeta is fully lined for extra support. Nylon Leno side sections mold firmly. Fagotted bias elastic hipline for perfect fit, prevents riding up. Acetate Satin down-stretch back panel. Convenient side zipper. How to Measure, Pg. 226. Postpaid. State waist, hips.
Fits average hip sizes 8-10 inches larger than waist.
Color: White. Waists: 26, 27, 28, 29, 30, 31, 32, 33, 34, 36, 38 in.
32 AP 6266—Av. lgth.: 14 in. waist down; 2 in. above waist. $8.95
32 AP 6295—Long lgth.: 16 in. waist down; 2 in. above waist. $8.95

SPIRAL-X FOR THE FIRMEST CONTROL 7.95

(B) COILWIRE BONED BACK FOR SUPPORT. Amazing new comfort in the most controlling Spiral-X design. Coilwire slims hips with new-found ease. Spiral-X front innershield of crossed, flexible wire will never poke tummy, keeps a flattened line. 3-section front panel of Rayon-figured Cotton Jacquard. Leno elastic side sections with shaped hip panels for added control. Non-roll elastic waist is coilwire-boned. Convenient side zipper.
Fits average hips 8-10 inches larger than waist.
Av. lgth.: 15 in. waist down; 2½ in. above. To Measure, Pg. 226.
Color: White. Waists: 30, 31, 32, 33, 34, 36, 38, 40, 42, 44 inches.
32 AP 6228—State waist, hip sizes. Postpaid.................$7.95

SPIRAL-X SLIMMING NON-ROLL WAIST 6.95

(C) NEW PANTY GIRDLE to match the popular Spiral-X non-roll top Girdle. Non-poke Spiral-X innershield for the most comfortable tummy slimming you've ever known. Cross-stretch Leno elastic sides and fagotted panels for special hip control. Down-stretch Rayon Satin elastic back slims contours. Figured Rayon-Cotton Brocade front panel. 3-inch non-roll elastic waistband trims midriff. Panty: Nylon Tricot crotch. To Measure, Pg. 226. Postpaid.
Fits average hips 8-10 inches larger than waist.
White. Waists: 26, 27, 28, 29, 30, 31, 32, 33, 34, 36 in. Garters detach.
32AP6255—Panty. Av. lgth.: 15 in. waist down; 2 above waist. $6.95
White. Waists: 26, 27, 28, 29, 30, 31, 32, 33, 34, 36, 38. State waist, hips.
32 AP 6253—Girdle. Av. lgth.: 15 in. waist down; 2 in. above. $6.95
32 AP 6263—Girdle. Long: 16 in. waist down; 2 in. above . . . $6.95

SPIRAL-X BASIC FOR EVERYDAY WEAR 5.95

(D) WAISTLINE SPIRAL-X. Wonderful new tummy control, with the spiral bones of innershield flattening and smoothing in comfort—will never poke. Side sections of firm Leno elastic, with bias elastic at the hipline for the most figure-flattering fit. Figured Rayon-Cotton Jacquard front panel. Down-stretch Acetate Satin lastex back panel to diminish hips smoothly. Convenient side zipper. Elasticized waistline. Measuring Instructions on Pg. 226.
Fits average hips 8-10 inches larger than waist.
Average Length: 14½ inches from the waist down.
Color: White. Waists: 26, 27, 28, 29, 30, 31, 32, 33, 34, 36 inches.
32 AP 6237—State waist, hip sizes. Postpaid $5.95

FAMOUS CONTOUR CONTROL INNERSHIELD TO FLATTEN ABDOMEN SMOOTHLY

HIGH-WAIST CINCHER 8.95

(E) A SMOOTH PRINCESS LINE. 4-inch cross-stretch elastic waistband; plush-lined non-roll bones to slim midriff. Boned Contour Control innershield trims abdomen. Rayon Satin front and hip panels, plus 4 Leno elastic sections to sleek silhouette. Comfortable down-stretch Rayon Satin elastic back for ease. White. To Measure, Pg. 226. State waist, hips.
Fits av. hips 8-10 in. larger than waist.
Waists: 26, 27, 28, 29, 30, 31, 32, 33, 34, 36 inches.
32 AP 6212—Av. lgth.: 14½ in. from waist down;
4 inches above.
216 WARDS CBASDEPO   Postpaid . . . $8.95

WAIST CINCHER CORSELET 9.95

(F) NEW SLIMNESS. Cross-stretch elastic Cinch Band plus Contour Control innershield to flatten tummy. "Glamorise" lift-action Bra for flattery. 4 Leno elastic panels. Figured Rayon-Cotton Batiste front, back and sides complete firm, molded contour.
Fits av. hips 3-4½ in. larger than bust.
Av.-full Bust: 34, 35, 36, 37, 38, 39, 40, 42, 44.
32 AP 7385—Fits av. figures. Average length: 25 inches; 15 in. from waist down. Postpaid.
32 AP 7386—Fits short-waisted figures. Short Lgth.: 22 in.; 13 in. waist down. Postpaid.
Color: White. State bust, waist, hips . . $9.95

"HURDLE GIRDLE" 6.95

(G) WALK IN COMFORT. Criss-cross front panels of Rayon Satin are cut to allow leg action freedom. Lightly boned front trims tummy. 4-sections of cross-stretch Leno elastic plus down-stretch Rayon Satin back mold figure smoothly. High 3-in. non-roll elastic to taper waist. Convenient side zipper. How to Measure, Pg. 226. Color: White.
Fits av. hips 8-10 in. larger than waist.
Waists: 26, 27, 28, 29, 30, 31, 32, 33, 34, 36, 38, 40.
32AP6204—Av.: 14 in. waist down; 2 in. above.
32AP6246—Long: 16 in. down; 2 in. above.
State waist, hip sizes. Postpaid $6.95

"GOLDEN TOUCH" 5.95

(H) ACCENT ON GLAMOUR. Rayon Power Net Step-in has tummy-flattening V-cut overlay with gold-colored trim. Gently shapes figure to sleek new slimness. 2-in. non-roll elastic band trims waistline. Nylon Tricot crotch on Panty; inner crotch detaches to launder. To Measure, Pg. 226.
Fits av. hips 8-10 in. larger than waist.
Waists: Sm. (24-26); M. (27-28); L. (29-30); Ex. Lge. (31-32). State waist, hips, color.
32AP6397—Panty. Av. lgth.: 14 in.; 2 above.
32AP6398—Girdle. Av. lgth.: 14 in.; 2 above.
Colors: Black, White. Postpaid $5.95

The Spiral-x girdles from *Montgomery Ward* features metal coil bones "that can't poke."

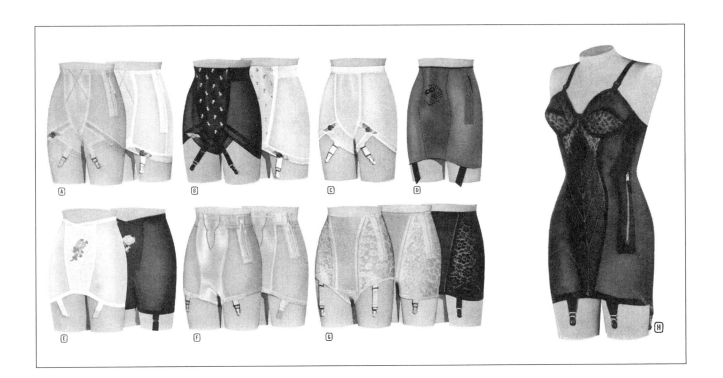

Nylon power net girdles for "lightweight control" from *Montgomery Ward*.

Although this girdle from the *Montgomery Ward* catalog had no bones, it firmly controlled the body with power net, rayon satin elastic panels, and a zipper.

Nationally Known for High-style, Fine-fit

Girdles in black, blue, white, pink, and red from the 1956–57 *Montgomery Ward* catalog.

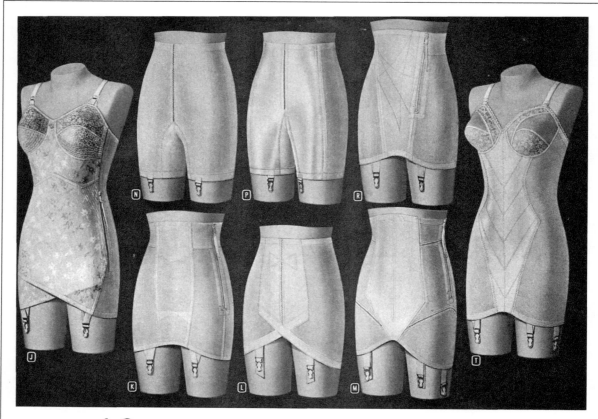

Nationally-known, Selected for Style and Slimming

WARNER'S . . . BESTFORM . . . YOUTHCRAFT . . . SIL-O-ETTE . . . FLEXEES. SENT TO YOU POSTPAID

BESTFORM'S "FLIRTATION WALK" CORSELET 10.00

[J] Criss-cross front panels of Rayon and Cotton Brocade release legs for new walking comfort. Full-length Leno elastic sides smooth silhouette; back waist gore for ease. Down-stretch Rayon Satin back molds a controlled line. Defined midriff flatters figure. Embroidered Nylon Sheer at bust, lined and stitched for positive uplift. Convenient side zipper; hooks at bust. How to Measure, Pg. 226. Color: White. Postpaid.

Fits average hips 3-4½ inches larger than bust.

Average Length: 25 in.; 15 in. from waist down. State bust, waist, hips.
32AP7367–Av. Bust: B Cup: 32, 33, 34, 35, 36, 37, 38, 39, 40, 42, 44 . .$10.00

CRISS-CROSS CONTROL GIRDLE 5.95

[K] Criss-cross elastic bands under a smooth Nylon Taffeta front panel create boneless, comfortable control, flatten tummy skillfully. Cross-stretch Nylon Leno elastic sides slim hipline. Rayon Satin down-stretch back molds a flattering curve. Flexible Coilwire boned non-roll elastic waistband fits high, smoothes away the inches. Convenient side zipper. Check Joan Browne Measuring Instructions on Page 226. Color: White.

Fits average hips 8-10 inches larger than waist.

Waists: 26, 27, 28, 29, 30, 31, 32, 34, 36. Av. Lgth.: 14 in.; 2 in. above waist.
32 AP 6290–State waist and hip sizes. Postpaid $5.95

YOUTHCRAFT 7.95 AND 8.95

[L] "Cut-up" gives you more leg-action freedom. Shaped at the front for wonderful ease when you walk. Elastic tape at lower edge is non-binding, stretches with every move. Slimming Nylon Power Net sides trim hips smoothly. Extra tummy control with concealed Rayon Satin elastic front panel. Down-stretch Rayon elastic back panel molds a slim contour. Nylon Tricot crotch on Panty. Joan Browne Measuring Instructions on Page 226. Postpaid.

Fits av. hips 8-10 in. larger than waist.

White. Waists: S. (24-26); Med. (27-28); Lge. (29-30); Ex. Lge. (31-32). State waist, hips. Lgth. on body: Girdle: 14 in.; Panty, 15 in.
32 AP 6324–Girdle $7.95
32 AP 6326–Panty. Garters detach. . .$8.95

FIGURAMA BY FLEXEES 12.95

[M] A new concept in foundation design. Nylon Leno lastique side sections, with unique stretch to duplicate muscle action for flattering, comfortable control. Down-stretch Nylon Satin elastic back panel, plus lined Nylon Satin front panel, combine to mold a fashionable trim silhouette. High, slimming waist is cut for superb fit, with light non-roll boning. Cross-stretch insert at back waist for comfort. Convenient side zipper for dressing ease. Check Joan Browne Measuring Instructions on Page 226. Sent Postpaid.

Fits av. hips 8-10 in. larger than waist.

White. Waists: 26, 28, 30, 32, 34, 36 inches.
Av. Length: 14 in. waist down; 2 in. above.
32AP6366–State waist, hips. $12.95

ALL-ELASTIC SIL-O-ETTE 4.50 TO 6.95

[N] [P] Lightweight Leno elastic Step-ins, now available in Extra Sizes. Patented Rayon Tricot crotch contour-cut for non-binding fit. Long-stretch elastic tapers waist, hips and thighs in boneless control. Garters detach. To Measure, Pg. 226. Postpaid.
Av. Lgth.: 14½ in. waist down. State waist, hips.

Order Size	34	36	38	40	42
To Fit Hips	33-34	35-36	37-38	39-40	41-43

Order Size	44	46	48	50
To Fit Hips	43-44	45-46	47-48	49-50

(N) "SPORT TIGHTS". White. All Leno elastic.
32 AP 6365–Reg. Hip Sizes: 34, 36, 38, 40, 42 in. .$4.50
32 AP 6363–Extra Hip Sizes: 44, 46, 48, 50 in. . .$5.95
(P) "DRESS TIGHTS". White. Rayon Satin front panel.
32 AP 6359–Reg. Hip Sizes: 34, 36, 38, 40, 42 in. .$5.50
32 AP 6353–Extra Hip Sizes: 44, 46, 48, 50 in. . . .$6.95

WARNER'S FINE FOUNDATIONS FOR EVERY FIGURE NEED 8.95 TO 16.50

[R] Firm, controlled hipline molding, with supple Leno elastic panels slimming away the inches. Lustrous Rayon-Cotton Batiste front panel, with separate boned innershield to whittle tummy. Rayon Satin down-stretch back panel completes the figure control. 2-in. non-roll elastic waistband slims the midriff line. Convenient side zipper. See Measuring Instructions, Page 226. Postpaid.

Fits av. hips 8-10 in. larger than waist.

White. Waist Sizes: 28, 29, 30, 31, 32, 34 inches.
32 AP 6203–Average Length: 14 inches from the waist down; 2 inches above the waist.
32 AP 6202–Short Length: 12 inches from the waist down; 2 inches above the waist.
State waist and hip sizes. Postpaid $8.95

[T] Achieve a slender, smooth sheath line from bosom to thigh. Plunging Bra of embroidered Nylon Marquisette and Nylon Sheer gives youthful uplift. All-elastic Step-in design, with figure-molding Nylon Power Net side sections. Down-stretch Rayon Satin elastic front and back panels for controlled slimming. Diagonal seaming flattens tummy. Proportioned in regular and half sizes for fit. To Measure, Pg. 226.

Fits av. hips 3-4½ in. larger than bust.

White. Av. Lgth.: 25 in.; 15 in. from waist down.
32AP7370–Av.: B Cup: 34, 35, 36, 37, 38, 39, 40 in.
32AP7371–Full: C Cup: 34, 35, 36, 37, 38, 39, 40 in.
32AP7372–Short-waisted figures. Av.: B Cup: 34, 35, 36, 37, 38, 39, 40. Lgth.: 24 in.; 15 in. waist down. State waist, hips. Postpaid . . .$16.50

[U] Proportioned in half sizes to put your waistline where it belongs. Available in average and long lengths for proper fit and control. Pre-shrunk (max. shrink. 5%). Cotton Batiste with boned innershield to flatten tummy. Fabric back plus Leno elastic sides slim contours. Gracefully rounded bust; Nylon Marquisette trim. To Measure, Pg. 226.

Fits av. hips 4-6 in. larger than bust.

Average Length: 24 in.; 15 in. waist down.
32AP7381–Av.: B Cup: 35, 36, 37, 38, 39, 40, 41, 42.
32AP7382–Full: C Cup: 36, 37, 38, 39, 40, 41, 42.

Fits av.-full hips 4-6 in. larger than bust.

Long Length: 25 in.; 16 in. from waist down.
32AP7380–Av.: B Cup: 36, 37, 38, 39, 40, 41, 42.
White. State bust, waist, hips. Postpaid $15.00

[U]

ALL WARDS 221

Higher end girdles sold through *Montgomery Ward*. They sold for $4.50 to $16.50.

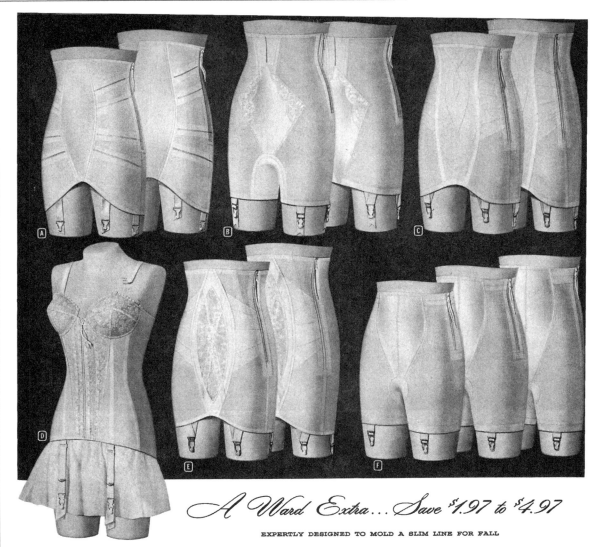

A Ward Extra... Save $1.97 to $4.97

EXPERTLY DESIGNED TO MOLD A SLIM LINE FOR FALL

- NOW EXTRA SPECIAL SAVINGS . . . for you on High Fashion Waist-slimmers.
- HIGH QUALITY . . . Laboratory approved elastics, fabrics; workmanship.
- EXPERT DETAILING . . . Joan Browne styling assures complete satisfaction.
- PROPORTIONED LENGTHS, MANY SIZES . . . offer custom fit, comfort.
- COILWIRE BONING . . . molds — will not poke or pinch; slims beautifully.
- SLENDERIZING . . . balanced-stretch elastic for more figure flattery.

SLENDERIZING FIGURE BUILDER 8.98 2 Lgths.

[A] Save $2.00. Sells in manufacturer's line for $10.98. Bias Bands of firm Leno elastic control stretch to flatten the tummy, slim hips and thighs. Wear it a high 3 inches above the waist to gently mold midriff. Coilwire non-roll bones never poke or pinch. Rayon Satin elastic down-stretch front and back panels slim your figure. Cross-stretch elastic at back waist. Convenient side zipper. 6 garters. Measuring Instructions on Pg. 226. Ship. wt. 1 lb. 4 oz.
Color: White. Waists: 27, 28, 29, 30, 31, 32, 33, 34, 36 inches.
Fits average hips 8-10 inches larger than waist.
32 A 6226—*Average Length:* 14 inches waist down; 3 above.
Fits average to full hips 9-11 inches larger than waist.
32 A 6287—*Long Length:* 16 inches waist down; 3 in. above.
Please state waist and hip measurements $8.98

FRONT ZIPPER TORSOLETTE B, C, D CUPS 8.98

[D] Save $2.00. Sells nationally for $10.98. Specially designed to mold a smooth midriff, flatten tummy and control hipline. Perfect choice for the new and narrow silhouette. Generous sections of Leno elastic at sides and back for trim, comfortable fit. Coilwire bones throughout will not poke or pinch. Firm Nylon Taffeta front panel. Nylon Sheer bust section has flattering under-bust wire, may be worn strapless or in five versatile decolleté styles. Convenient front zipper for dressing ease. How to Measure, Page 226.
Length: 10 inches from the waist down. *Color:* White.
32 A 7375—*Average:* B Cup: 32, 34, 36, 38, 40, 42 inches.
32 A 7376—*Full:* C Cup: 34, 36, 38, 40, 42, 44, 46 inches.
32 A 7377—*Extra Full:* D Cup: 34, 36, 38, 40, 42, 44, 46 inches.
Ship. wt. 14 oz. *State bust, waist, hip sizes* $8.98

DACRON LENO ELASTIC 6.98 AND 7.98 2 Lgths.

[B] Save $1.97 on Girdle, $2.97 on Panty. Similar quality sells nationally for $8.95. All elastic with balanced stretch to take inches off hips, flatten tummy, and smooth midriff. Diamond panels of Rayon Satin elastic at front and back with Dacron Leno elastic for fine fit, plus wearing ease. Coilwire boning at waist and convenient side zipper are plush lined for wearing ease. Panty is cut long to slim hips, has soft Rayon Tricot crotch. How to Measure, Pg. 226. Ship. wt. 12 oz. *Please state waist and hip measurements.*
Fits average hips 8-10 inches larger than waist.
Color: White. Waists: 26, 27, 28, 29, 30, 31, 32, 34 inches.
32A6315—Panty: *Av. Lgth.:* 14 in. waist down; 3 above. $7.98
32A6317—Panty: *Long:* 16 in. waist down; 3 in. above . . $7.98
32A6314—Girdle: *Long:* 16 in. waist down; 3 in. above . . $6.98

DACRON HI-WAIST GIRDLE 7.98 2 Lgths.

[E] Save $2.97. Sells nationally for $10.95. Features finest quality workmanship. Reinforced Power bands combine with fully lined Dacron Taffeta front to take inches off hips and hold a flat line over tummy. Four sections of Leno elastic for effective hip control plus slimming down-stretch Rayon Satin elastic back panel. High waist with Leno elastic back yoke for wonderful midriff trimming. Coilwire boned for comfortable waistline control. Six trolley garters. Measuring Instructions are on Page 226.
Fits average to full hips 8-11 inches larger than waist.
Color: White. Waists: 27, 28, 29, 30, 31, 32, 34, 36 inches.
32 A 6217—*Average Lgth.:* 14 inches waist down; 3 above.
32 A 6221—*Long Lgth.:* 16 inches waist down; 3 in. above.
Ship. wt. 1 lb. *State waist, hip measurements* $7.98

NYLON TAFFETA FITS WAIST SIZES TO 42 6.98

[C] Save $3.97. Similar quality sells in manufacturer's line for $10.95. Slimming features: fits 3 inches above waist to smooth midriff; the Nylon Taffeta front panel is lightly boned for expert control; Power bands of reinforced Leno elastic for extra control; Leno elastic sections slim hips comfortably; Rayon Satin down-stretch back assures you of a smooth and slender silhouette. Flexible Coilwire boning at high waist for comfortable control and a slim waist without poking. Joan Browne Measuring Instructions on Page 226.
Fits average to full hips 8-11 inches larger than waist.
Color: White. Waists: 28, 29, 30, 31, 32, 34, 36, 38, 40, 42 in.
32 A 6250—*Average Length:* 14 in. waist down; 3 above.
32 A 6254—*Long Length:* 16 in. waist down; 3 in. above.
Ship. wt. 1 lb. *State waist, hip measurements* $6.98

BONELESS ALL ELASTIC THIGH CONTROL 5.98

[F] Save $4.97. Similar quality sells nationally for $10.95. Nylon Tricot contour crotch designed for superb fit, shaped for greater comfort. Rayon Satin elastic front and back with cross-stretch Leno elastic sides for two-way control that molds a slim, trim line. Cut long on leg for a smooth and controlled thigh line. Woven elastic waistband ensures snug fit without binding. Convenient side zipper. Ideal Panty choice for sportswear. To Measure, see Page 226.
Fits average to full hips 8-11 inches larger than waist.
Color: White. Waists: 26, 27, 28, 29, 30, 31, 32, 33, 34 inches.
32 A 6323—*Average Length:* 14 in. waist down; 1½ in. above.
32 A 6321—*Short Lgth.:* 13 in. waist down; 1½ in. above.
32 A 6325—*Long Length:* 16 in. waist down; 1½ in. above.
Ship. wt. 11 oz. *State waist and hip sizes* $5.98

222 WARDS ALL

FOR JOAN BROWNE MEASURING INSTRUCTIONS, CONSULT PAGE 226. WARDS CONVENIENT MONTHLY PAYMENT PLAN IS EXPLAINED ON INSIDE BACK COVER

Featuring spiral boning, nylon, and zippers, these
Montgomery Ward girdles offered more definite shaping.

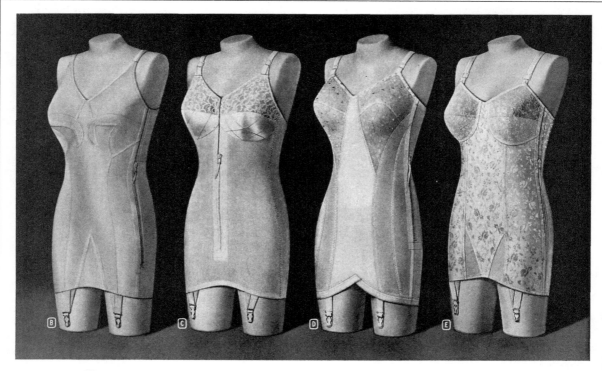

Proportioned to Fit Regular, Half-size, Tall Figures

SLIMMING DUAL CONTROL...DOWN-STRETCH BACK...CROSS-STRETCH SIDES

- PERFECTLY BALANCED STRETCH...cross-stretch sides plus down-stretch back.
- SKILLFULLY BONED PANELS...flatten abdomen for smooth longline control.
- FLATTERING BUST SECTIONS...mold rounded contours, give comfortable uplift.
- FINE FABRICS...coupled with careful styling and expert workmanship.
- PROPERLY SIZED...to fit your particular figure requirements accurately.
- LABORATORY APPROVED...to assure satisfactory fit `plus proper control.

Send all measurements requested; check instructions on Page 226. It's easy to Shop by Mail at Wards; turn to Page 1138.

HALF SIZES

A Half-Size figure is shorter from shoulder to waist than average figure. Height, weight do not determine half-size.

POWER BAND CONTROL 9.98

(A) Styled for superb hip control, this flattering Corselet fits regular or half-size (short-waisted) figures. Nylon Power net elastic at side front is reinforced, diagonally stitched to flatten abdomen, whittle hips. Boned Rayon Satin front panel and Rayon Satin side panels assure firm control. Down-stretch Rayon Satin elastic back smooths a flattering line. Full-length two-way stretch Nylon Power net sides. Power net back waist yoke for the finest fit, greater comfort. Nylon Marquisette bust section has Rayon Satin undercups for firm uplift. Elastic insert at adjustable straps. Side zipper; hooks at bust. Joan Browne Measuring Instructions given on Pg. 226. Shipping weight 1 lb. 2 oz. Color: Pink.

Av. Busts: 34, 35, 36, 37, 38, 39, 40, 42, 44 in.
Fits average hips 3-4½ in. larger than bust.
32 A 7361—Fits *Average* figures. *Average Length:* about 25 inches; 15 inches waist down.
32 A 7362—Fits *Short-waisted* figures. *Short Length:* about 22 inches; 13 inches waist down.
State bust, waist, hip measurements......**$9.98**

BUILT-UP BUST FLATTERS FULL FIGURES 9.98

(B) Three-way longline control. Boned Rayon Satin front panel flattens abdomen. Cross-stretch Batiste elastic side panels slim hips. Firm down-stretch Batiste elastic back controls with comfort (sketch, left). Built-up bust section is uniquely cut to mold a flattering line and to smooth excess flesh. Rayon Satin built-up back has elastic gore for comfort. Convenient side zipper; hooks at bust. For best possible fit, check Measuring Instructions, Page 226. Color: Pink.

Full Bust Sizes: 36, 38, 40, 42, 44, 46 inches.
Fits av. hips 3-4½ in. larger than bust.
32A7348—Fits *Average* figures. *Average Length:* about 25 inches; 15 inches from waist down.
Fits small hips 1-2½ in. larger than bust.
32A7345—Fits *Short-waisted* figures. *Short Length:* about 22 inches; 13 inches from the waist down.

Full Bust Sizes: 38, 40, 42, 44, 46, 48 inches.
Fits full hips 5-7 inches larger than bust.
32 A 7347—Fits *Heavier* figures. *Long Length:* about 27 inches; 17 inches from the waist down.
Ship. wt. 1 lb. 5 oz. State bust, waist, hip sizes...........**$9.98**

ALL LENO ELASTIC 7.98

(C) Maximum control with minimum weight—designed especially for fuller figures. All-way stretch Leno elastic comfortably molds, flexibly controls, yet allows complete freedom of body movement. Boned, lined Cotton Coutil innershield smoothly flattens abdomen. Well-designed bust section provides a wide separation, molds gracefully rounded contours. Attractive Alencon-type lace at upper bust; lustrous Rayon Satin lower bust is diamond-stitched for firm and flattering uplift. Convenient front zipper, with hook-and-eye closing at bust. Adjustable Satin shoulder straps have forked elastic inserts. Measure carefully, according to directions given on Page 226, to assure comfortable fit and control. Ship. wt. 1 lb. 4 oz. Color: White.

Fits av.-full hips 4-6 in. larger than bust.
Av.-Full Busts: 36, 38, 40, 42, 44, 46, 48 in.
32A7335—Fits *Av.-Full* figures. *Av. to Long Length:* about 26 in.; 15½ in. waist down.
32A7334—Fits *Short-waisted* figures. *Short Length:* abt. 22 in.; 13 in. from waist down.
State bust, waist, hip sizes...........**$7.98**

CRISS-CROSS CONTROL 7.98

(D) Proportioned Sizes slim average, short-waisted or long figures. Criss-cross elastic innershield smooths abdomen comfortably without bones. Nylon Taffeta front and hip panels, plus 4 sections of cross-stretch Leno elastic for firm figure molding. Rayon Satin down-stretch elastic back combines control with comfort. Princess style embroidered Nylon Sheer bust section is fully lined for flattering uplift. Woven elastic band at lower front won't bind when walking or sitting. Straps: elastic inserts at back. Side zipper; hooks at bust. How to Measure, Pg. 226. Color: White.

Av. Busts: 36, 37, 38, 39, 40, 42, 44, 46 inches.
Fits av. hips 3-4½ in. larger than bust.
32A7392-Fits *Average* figures. *Average Lgth.:* about 25 inches; 15 inches from waist down.
32A7391—Fits *Short-waisted* figures. *Short Length:* abt. 22 inches; 13 in. waist down.
Fits av.-full hips 4-6 in. larger than bust.
Av.-Full Busts: 36, 37, 38, 39, 40, 42, 44, 46 in.
32A7393—Fits *Heavier* figures. *Long Length:* 27 inches; 17 inches from the waist down.
Ship. wt. 1 lb. State bust, waist, hips....**$7.98**

COTTON-RAYON JACQUARD 5.98

(E) For new flattery—a fashion Corselet in fine Cotton and Rayon Jacquard. Proportioned to fit both Average and Half-size (short-waisted) figures. Check these quality features of higher priced corselets. Embroidered Nylon sheer bust section, fully lined to give flattering rounded contours. Adjustable Nylon shoulder straps with elastic inserts for more comfort. Rayon Satin elastic down-stretch back with cross-stretch yoke at waist for fine fit. Firmly woven Leno elastic side sections for firm hip control; front gores for walking ease. Separate boned innershield gives added control over abdomen. Send all measurements; see Page 226 for Measuring Instructions.

Color: White. Shipping weight 1 lb. 2 oz.
Fits av. hips 3-4½ in. larger than bust.
Average Busts: 34, 35, 36, 37, 38, 39, 40, 42, 44.
32 A 7316—Fits *Average* figures. *Average Length:* about 25 in.; 15 in. waist down.
32 A 7315—Fits *Short-waisted* figures. *Short Length:* about 21 in.; 12½ in. waist down.
State bust, waist, hip measurements...**$5.98**

228 WARDS CR&SDKFO

BE SURE TO CHECK WARDS FLATTERING HALF-SIZE FASHIONS STARTING ON PAGE 81. CONVENIENT CREDIT TERMS ARE LISTED INSIDE BACK COVER.

Girdles featuring boning, zippers, and "power band" control, from the Fall & Winter 1956–57 *Montgomery Ward* catalog.

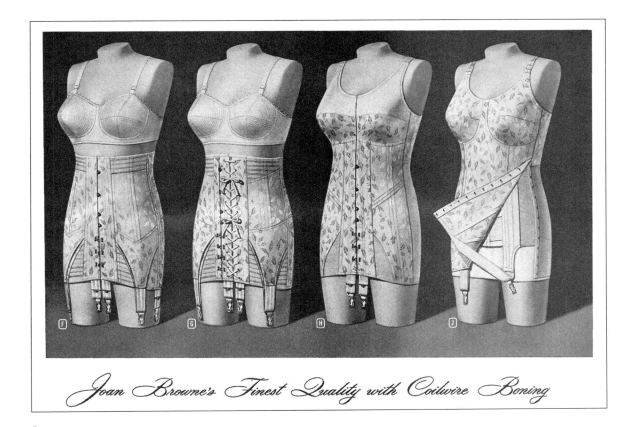

Joan Browne's Finest Quality with Coilwire Boning

For "troublesome" figures, these well boned girdles from *Montgomery Ward* hearken back to an earlier era, featuring lacing, metal clasps, and coil wire boning.

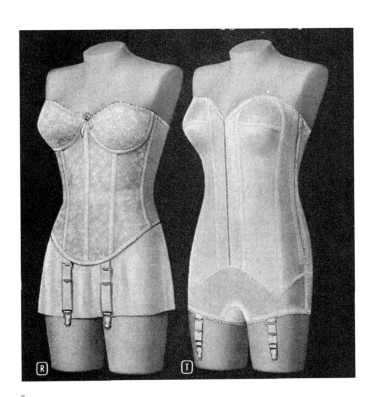

Montgomery Ward called these "waist cinchers" or "bracelettes."

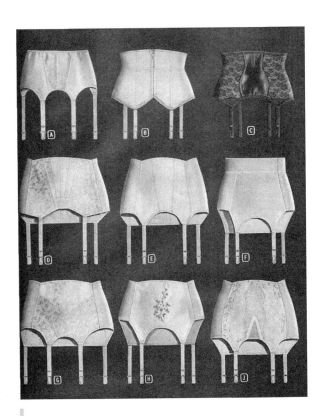

Waist whittlers with bones and elastic, from the *Montgomery Ward* 1956–57 catalog.

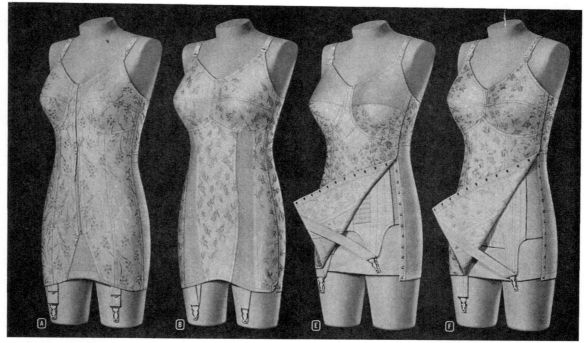

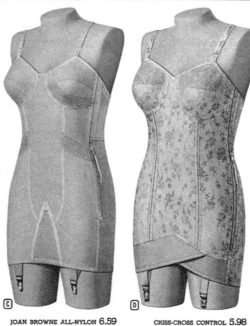

All-in-one-flattery

EXPERT DESIGNS TO SLIM, SUPPORT IN 3 LGTHS.

WARDS SELECTION OF CORSELETS WITH 3 TYPES OF ABDOMINAL CONTROL

1. Built-in innershields give abdominal control without bulk of extra innershield (A and B).
2. Lightly boned, lined front panel or criss-cross inner elastic give gentle control (C and D).
3. Boned innerbelts give firm abdominal support to figures demanding more control (E and F).

PATENTED BUILT-IN INNERSHIELDS 8.98

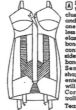

[A] Similar quality sells nationally for $15.00. The exclusive, patented front panel and built-in belt close with one pull of the zipper. Bulkless innerbelt has criss-cross elastic to lift the abdomen; boned front panel flattens and controls. Cross-stretch elastic sides and gores slim the hips; boned back smooths contours. Semi-built-up bust section shapes a flattering uplift. Patented non-slip shoulder straps will not cut. Cotton and Rayon Corset Batiste, firmly controlling. To Measure, Page 226.

Tearose. Ship. wt. 1 lb. 10 oz.

Av. to full Busts: 36, 37, 38, 39, 40, 41, 42, 44, 46, 48 in.

Fits average to full hips 4-6 in. larger than bust.

32 A 7130—*Average Length:* 26 in.; 15 in. waist down.
32 A 7147—*Long Length:* 28 in.; 17 in. waist down.

Fits small hips 1-2½ in. larger than bust.

32 A 7149—*Average Length:* 26 in.; 15 in. waist down.
State bust, waist and hip measurements.......$8.98

EVEN-PUL 5.95 AND 6.95

[B] Smooth or Laced Back Corselets with special contour control innershield. Boned Cotton Coutil with elastic sections flattens abdomen and diaphragm. Semi-built-up 2-section bust lifts and supports fuller figures. Elastic side sections and gores combined with sturdy Cotton and Rayon Corset Batiste to slim hips and back. See Page 226 for Measuring. Postpaid.

Tearose. *State bust, waist, hip sizes.*

Av.-full hips 4-6 in. over bust.

SMOOTH BONED BACK. *Av. to Full Busts:* 36, 37, 38, 39, 40, 42, 44, 46 inches.

32 AP 7237—*Average Length:* 25 in.; 15 in. from waist down........$5.95
32 AP 7238—*Short Length:* 23 inches; 13 inches from waist down.....$5.95

LACED BONED BACK. Laces adjust easily for custom-like fit. *Av. to Full Busts:* 36, 38, 40, 42, 44, 46, 48, 50 inches.

32 AP 7239—*Average Length:* 25 in.; 15 in. from waist down........$6.95
32 AP 7240—*Short Length:* 23 inches; 13 inches from waist down.....$6.95

BONED INNERBELT FOR MOST ABDOMINAL SUPPORT

JOAN BROWNE ALL-NYLON 6.59

[C] Comfortable featherlight control molds smooth line from bust to thigh. 2-section bust has contour-stitched undercups for firm uplift. 3-section Nylon Taffeta front panel assures firmer control; the center panel is lightly boned, lined to flatten tummy. Cross-stretch Nylon Leno elastic side panels and gores trim hips, yet allow sitting, walking comfort. Firm Nylon back panel whittles a slim figure. To Measure, Pg. 226. Wt. 15 oz.

Pink or White. *State bust, waist, hips, color.*

Fits av. hips 3-4½ in. larger than bust.

Av. Busts: 32, 33, 34, 35, 36, 37, 38, 39, 40, 42in.

32A7354—*Av. Lgth.:* 25 in.; 15 in. waist down.
32A7353—*Short:* 23 in.; 13 in. waist down...$6.59

Full Busts: 34, 35, 36, 37, 38, 39, 40, 42 in.

32A7355—*Av. Lgth.:* 25 in.; 15 in. waist down.
32A7352—*Short:* 23 in.; 13 in. waist down...$6.59

CRISS-CROSS CONTROL 5.98

[D] Walk or sit in Easy-stride comfort... Bias cut elastic bands at lower front will never bind legs. All elastic innershield combines with boned back to hold a flatteringly smooth line. 2-section bust with lined Nylon Sheer upper cup uplifts and contours bustline. Slimming cross-stretch Leno elastic side sections, gores. Rayon and Cotton Batiste. Side zipper. To Measure, Pg. 226. Wt. 1 lb. 2 oz. White.

Average Busts: 34, 35, 36, 37, 38, 39, 40, 42in.

Av. hips 3-4½ inches larger than bust.

32A7175—*Av. Lgth.:* 24 in.; 14 in. waist down.

Full Busts: 34, 35, 36, 37, 38, 39, 40, 42 in.

Full hips 5-7 in. larger than bust.

32A7176—*Long Lgth.:* 25 in.; 16 in. waist down.

State bust, waist, hip measurements. $5.98

FOR SHORT-WAISTED FIGURES 6.98

[E] Proportioned for you who wear half-size dresses (shorter from shoulder to waist). Semi-built-up bust section with fused "Klex" interlining in lower cups to lift and round the bust; soft fabric upper bust. Cotton Poplin innerbelt has elastic reinforcements, is boned for firm abdominal control. Pre-shrunk (max. shrink. 3%) Rayon and Cotton Batiste with boned back for added support and smoother lines. Cross-stretch elastic side sections and gores slim hipline. How to Measure, Page 226. Ship. wt. 1 lb. 7 oz.

Color: Tearose only.

Fits av. hips 3-4½ in. larger than bust.

Average Busts: 34, 36, 38, 40, 42, 44, 46 in.

32 A 7016—Fits Short-waisted figures. *Average Length:* 24 inches; 14 inches waist down.

32 A 7015—Fits Short-waisted figures. *Short Length:* 20 inches; 12 inches waist down.

State bust, waist and hip sizes.........$6.98

JACQUARD 3.98   POPLIN 3.49

[F] Budget-priced side hook with boned Cotton Coutil innerbelt for abdominal control. Figure molding bust section for good uplift. Boned back supports and smooths back. Slimming elastic side sections and gores. To Measure, Page 226. Ship. wt. 1 lb. 7 oz.

Av. to Full Busts: 34, 36, 38, 40, 42, 44, 46, 48.

Fits av. hips 4-6 in. over bust.

BETTER COTTON AND RAYON JACQUARD. Sturdy fabric; semi-built-up top. Shown. Tearose.

32A7029—*Av. Lgth.:* 24 in.; 14 in. waist down.
32A7026—*Long:* 26 in.; 16 in. waist down.
*State bust, waist, hip measurements....$3.98

Fits av. hips 3-4½ in. larger than bust.

COTTON AND RAYON POPLIN. Not shown. Economy quality, with a bodice cut top. Tearose.

32A7027—*Av. Lgth.:* 23½ in.; 14in. waist down.
32A7022—*Short:* 21½ in.; 12 in. waist down.
*State bust, waist, hip measurements....$3.49

230 WARDS DPO   LABORATORY APPROVED, CREDIT TERMS, INSIDE BACK COVER.

These girdles had enough figure-shaping power that *Montgomery Ward* called them "corselets."

American Modern...
casual freedom of fashion today
for a naturally beautiful figure

Skippies
by
Formfit

Here is the girdle that suggests the shape . . . doesn't insist on having its own hard way with your figure. Result . . . a naturally beautiful line, achieved with the comfort and freedom of fashion today . . . American Modern. No wonder Skippies is America's favorite girdle. See why . . . be fitted in Skippies at your favorite store.

Formfit

DRESS BY MR. MORT · HAT—JOHN FREDERICS "CHARMER"

The light touch of slimming . . . Skippies Girdle No. 945. White or Black Nylon elastic net with tummy-trimming front panel, 2½-in. waistband. (Also available as Pantie No. 845) S.M.L. Ex. L. $6.50. Shown with "Thrill" Bra No. 587 in cotton. $2.50

THE FORMFIT COMPANY · CHICAGO · NEW YORK · CANADIAN PLANT. TORONTO

175

not a seam to cut you anywhere!
Silf Skin Pantie Girdle is so firm . . . so friendly . . . has no crotch seams to cut and bother, yet moulds and controls beautifully! Make the *"inside-out test"* and discover that only Silf Skin exclusive seamless knit is just as velvety smooth on the inside as it is on the outside—feels so good next to you. Full-fashioned . . . preshrunk in white, also in black. Nylon elastic, $5.95. Silk elastic, $10.95. As shown, $5

NOW AVAILABLE IN SILF SKIN'S SUPER CONTROL
An extra-firm knit that combines amazing support and spring-back with comfort! $5.95

Silf Skin

MAKE THE SILF SKIN "INSIDE-OUT" COMFORT TEST

9AM   7PM

AT ALL FINE STORES. FOR NEAREST ONE, WRITE DEPT. S-5, SILF SKIN, INC., 10 E. 38TH ST., N. Y. C. 16; OR 215 SPADINA AVE., TORONTO, CANADA

Although this girdle appears more restrictive than many others of the era, in 1957 the makers of Formfit promised it "doesn't insist on having its own hard way with your figure."

Most girdles had slit openings to make using the restroom easier, but this 1957 ad for the Silk Skin girdle bragged about "no crotch seams."

Lace and Lastex made up many girdles of the late 50s, such as
this one featured in the March 1957 issue of *Seventeen*.

Although claiming to be modern,
this 1957 Sleekette corset really
hearkened back to an earlier era,
with it's front clasps, long line, and
shoulder straps.

Obviously, the lady doesn't know

Perma·lift's Magic Oval Pantie

CAN'T RIDE UP—EVER!

Apparently the young lady strolling on your left doesn't know that "Perma·lift's" *
Magic Oval Pantie ** Can't Ride Up—Ever! And how can a girl relax when
her girdle won't stay put. But you can be comfortable all day, in a "Perma·lift"
Magic Oval Pantie. It will never ride or creep—rub or wrinkle. Be fitted today.

Pantie 3808—Nylon Power Net. In five colors. Only $5.
Bra 33—Circular stitched cups. In Dacron. $3.95.

*Reg. U. S. Pat. Off. · A product of A. Stein & Company · Chicago—New York—Los Angeles **Pat. No. 2,705,801*

Seventeen—May, 1957

Perma·lift
PANTIES
NO BONES ABOUT IT
STAYS UP WITHOUT STAYS

This 1957 Perma-lift ad calls it a pantie, but it's still a girdle. Made of nylon
power net, the makers promised wearers would be "comfortable all day."

"Designed for the outdoor girl," this 1957 ad proclaimed, the Wilco panty girdle was suitable for under bathing suits as well as for any part of the Summer wardrobe.

A lightweight girdle advertised in *Seventeen* magazine in May of 1957.

A 1957 Formfit girdle designed to "slim you gently from high waistband all the way to mid thigh...for a *naturally* beautiful look."

This 1957 Lewella's girdle was "unbelievably soft" because it contained "pure cosmetic lanolin for the ultimate in comfort and beauty."

it's true!

LEWELLA

fits you...and your budget too!

"Trim-'N-Slim" panty brief in Power Net with **removable crotch shield.** S, M, L, XL. $4.00 Bra in A-B-C cups. $1.50

AT LEADING DEPARTMENT AND SPECIALTY STORES

LEWEL MFG. CO., 180 MADISON AVE., NEW YORK 16

This Lewella ad appeared in the October 1957 edition of *Seventeen* magazine.

To avoid bulges between the bra and girdle, many corsets were made "all in one," like this girdle from 1957.

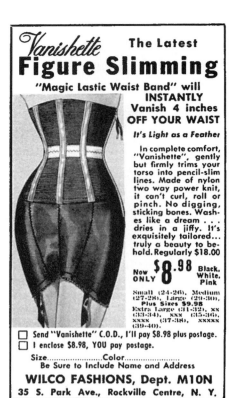
The '50s brought back the small waist, so many girdles began advertising the ability to take "inches off your waist." This girdle was featured in the November 1957 issue of *Seventeen*.

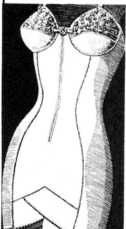

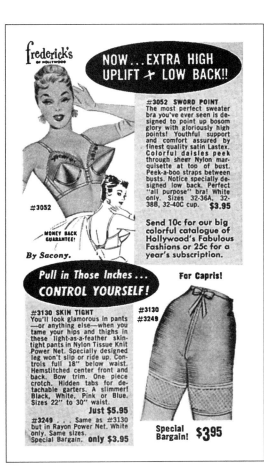

A unique girdle designed for wearing under tight pants, as seen in a 1958 issue of *Charm*.

A Wilco, zip-up girdle from 1958.

WHILE WAITING

DORA

Maternity-minded
Adjustable girdle and bra. Charma. White or black. Bra: nylon lace and leno-weave elastic of Dacron. 32 to 38 B, 32 to 40 C. About $6. Girdle: nylon power net, satin woven with elastic. S,M,L,XL. About $12
Lane Bryant, New York
The Maternity Shop, Boston

Adaptable slip
The slip with Helanca yarn inserts, that expand as you do. Lacy bodice and trim; adjustable shoulder straps. Expecto-Slip by Faerie. Nylon tricot and nylon lace. 32 to 42. About $6
Foley's, Houston
J. W. Robinson, Los Angeles

CHARM, July 1958

Victorian women wore corsets well into their pregnancies, and 1950s women often wore maternity girdles, as this 1958 girdle proves.

A Vassarette "extra long pantie girdle" made of nylon power net, from the September 1959 issue of *Ladies Home Journal*.

FOR
THAT
**MARDI
GRAS**
FEELING

GOSSARD'S

What fun to frolic... and figure right in your fashions,
too! **Answer** is the original design* with inner elastic bands
that gentle you in. Try on Answer. See how this
boneless wonder glamorizes *you*.

Left: **Answer Deb pantie**
  Featherweight style to put fun in function for debutante figures.
  Pantie with detachable garters $8.95. Matching girdle $7.95

Right: **Original Answer girdle**
  Takes a countdown on inches to make you svelte 'neath your
  splinter fashions. $10.95. Matching pantie $12.50

  Bra in embroidered cotton, contoured with foam rubber $3.95

*U.S. PAT. #2,803,822

©1959, THE H. W. *Gossard* CO., CHICAGO

Gossard's was a popular line of women's underwear in 1959.

A "full figure" girdle with firm control from 1959 by Vassarette.

Vassarette's "all-elastic knit girdle" from 1959.

A nylon powernet pantie girdle from 1959, by Vassarette.

Vassarette's "Stay There" pantie girdle from a 1959 issue of *Ladies' Home Journal*.

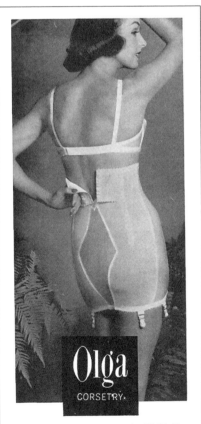

An adjustable waist girdle by Olga. It sold for $16.50 in 1959.

404359

something
magical
happens
in
Moon-Lite

For the newest in figure-wizardry—bring Moon-Lite romance into your life! The bare-minimum of a panty girdle begins bewitchery with moon-crescent inserts in just the right places to control—beautifully! Dipped waist...freedom-loving design—it's Moon-Lite enchantment no body can resist! White, Beige, Black. Small, Medium, Large. Girdle or Panty, $10.00. Matching bandeau, $5.00.

BIEN JOLIE

at fine stores or write...Bien Jolie, 16 E. 40 Street, New York 16, N.Y.

A "bare minimum" panty girdle in a "freedom loving design," costing $10 from Bien Jolie.

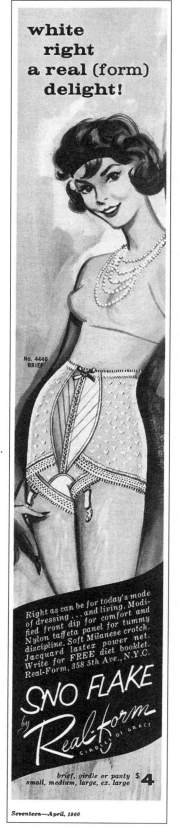

white
right
a real (form)
delight!

No. 4446
BRIEF

Right as can be for today's mode of dressing...and living. Modified front dip for comfort and Nylon taffeta panel for tummy discipline. Soft Milanese crotch. Jacquard lastex power net. Write for FREE diet booklet. Real-Form, 358 5th Ave., N.Y.C.

SNO FLAKE
by Real-Form
GIRDLE of GRACE

brief, girdle or panty $4
small, medium, large, ex. large

Seventeen—April, 1960

This Real-form girdle is typical of 1960, with a nylon tummy control panel and attached garters.

ONE OF
THE
NICEST
SURPRISES
IN YOUR
LIFE...

Surprise
bra and girdle

LONGLEG PANTIE—nylon lace and powernet —removable crotch shield #911, S, M, L, XL, White — $12.50

MATCHING LACE CONTOUR BRA #701, A,B,C cups $3.95

At better stores or write
SURPRISE BRASSIERE CO., INC.
102 Madison Ave., N. Y. 16, N. Y.

5 LENGTHS

Seventeen—April, 1960

A long line panty girdle by Surprise Brassiere Co., Inc.